YEAR OF DISCOVERY

ANNE ROONEY

ILLUSTRATED BY CHARLOTTE FARMER

THIS BOOK BELONGS TO

_____

Kane Miller
A DIVISION OF EDC PUBLISHING

HELLO, BUDDING GENIUS!

Life is an experiment, and this book is a space to record your ingenious ideas, wild theories, and original designs.

Inside, there are 365 STEM-themed activities. That's one for **EVERY DAY OF THE YEAR**. They'll take you out into space, around the natural world, back in time to spy on scientists, and into the workings of machines and other inventions. You'll explore how the universe works and discover your own ideas. Some activities will only take a minute, while others might take much longer. You can complete them in any order—just pick one that appeals to you, and get started!

JUST REMEMBER:

1. BE BOLD—imagination is key in STEM, so don't hesitate to think outside of the box!

2. Know that there are **NO** wrong answers or bad ideas. Many of the world's best discoveries came about by accident or mistake.

3. Have fun! **ENJOY** discovering fascinating facts on every page.

4. Once you're done, you'll have a **ONE-OF-A-KIND** record of your year.

BEFORE YOU GET STARTED ...

You don't need many materials to complete this journal; just a pen, pencil, and some colorful crayons or markers will do the trick.

But here are some other useful tools that you might like to use, too:

· A dictionary to help you check the exact spelling and meaning of words.

· A computer to further your research and understanding of ideas you discover in this book.

 If you're worried about changing your mind, or if you want more space to write or draw, you can use another piece of paper and stick it into the book.

 Remember, it doesn't matter if you struggle to spell, color, or draw. This book is not about grades or getting things perfect—it's your journal, so don't hold back.

 You might want to use books or online resources to help you complete certain activities, or you may want to depend only on your imagination—it's up to you. If you do want to use the Internet, just make sure you have a grown-up's permission.

1.

THE NORTHERN AND SOUTHERN LIGHTS ARE HUGE SWIRLY PATTERNS
OF COLORFUL LIGHTS THAT APPEAR IN THE SKY NEAR THE NORTH AND
SOUTH POLES. ADD THEM TO THE SKY IN THIS SCENE.

2.

YOU'RE AN INVENTOR, AND YOU'VE DESIGNED A MACHINE TO DO A TASK
OR CHORE YOU DON'T LIKE. WHAT WILL YOUR MACHINE DO?

3.

SCIENTISTS THINK THE DINOSAURS WERE WIPED OUT WHEN A LARGE ASTEROID (A ROCKY OBJECT FROM SPACE) CRASHED INTO EARTH 65 MILLION YEARS AGO. YIKES! DRAW YOUR OWN ASTEROID HERE.

4.

WHAT IF NO ONE HAD EVER INVENTED THE WHEEL? WHAT THINGS WOULDN'T YOU BE ABLE TO DO? LIST YOUR ANSWERS.

5.

A SEESAW WILL BALANCE IF THE THINGS ON EACH END ARE THE SAME WEIGHT. WHAT WOULD A SEESAW LOOK LIKE WITH AN ELEPHANT ON ONE SIDE AND A MOUSE ON THE OTHER? DRAW IT HERE.

6.

WE GET IMPORTANT VITAMINS FROM THE FOODS WE EAT, ESPECIALLY FRUIT AND VEGETABLES. PICK YOUR FAVORITE FRUIT OR VEGETABLE AND WRITE A NOTE THANKING IT FOR KEEPING YOU HEALTHY!

7.

YOU DESIGN AN AMAZING NEW FEATURE FOR A SMARTPHONE. WHAT CAN IT DO?

8.

DRAW AS MANY CIRCLES AS YOU CAN INSIDE THIS TRIANGLE. RECORD HOW MANY YOU MANAGE TO SQUEEZE IN.

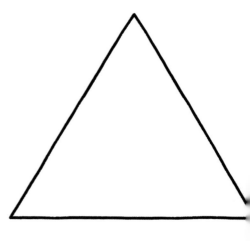

9.

OBJECTS ONLY WORK PROPERLY WHEN THEY'RE MADE OF THE RIGHT MATERIALS. FOR EXAMPLE, A TEAPOT HAS TO BE MADE OF SOMETHING HEATPROOF AND SOLID—IT CAN'T BE MADE OF GELATIN OR WOOL! WHICH MATERIALS WOULD OR WOULDN'T WORK FOR THE OBJECTS BELOW?

	DO USE:	DON'T USE:
A FORK		
A SWEATER		
A BOAT		

10.

DO YOU HAVE A FAVORITE NUMBER? WRITE IT BELOW—BUT WRITE IT AS MANY TIMES AS THE NUMBER ITSELF!

11.

SOME FOODS HAVE SPECIAL EFFECTS. FOR EXAMPLE, SCIENTISTS THINK THAT BEETS IMPROVE STAMINA, AND CHERRIES CAN HELP PREVENT MEMORY LOSS! PICK A FOOD AND GIVE IT A SPECIAL EFFECT.

12.

SCIENTISTS DON'T ALWAYS GET IT RIGHT! IN ANCIENT TIMES, THEY THOUGHT THAT DISEASES CAME FROM SMELLY AIR, WHICH THEY CALLED "MIASMA." TODAY, WE KNOW MANY DISEASES ARE CAUSED BY BACTERIA. MAKE UP A NEW THEORY OF YOUR OWN ABOUT ANYTHING YOU LIKE.

13.

YOU'RE A MAMMAL, SO YOU HAVE HAIR ON YOUR BODY. IF YOU WERE A BIRD, YOU WOULD HAVE FEATHERS. DRAW WHAT THAT WOULD LOOK LIKE!

14.

WHEN A VOLCANO ERUPTS, HOT GAS, LUMPS OF ROCK, ASH, AND LIQUID ROCK CALLED LAVA ALL BURST OUT. ADD AN ERUPTION TO THIS VOLCANO.

15.

GRAVITY IS A FORCE THAT PULLS EVERYTHING (INCLUDING YOU!) TO THE GROUND AND MAKES THINGS FALL DOWN. WHAT WOULD IT BE LIKE IF GRAVITY DISAPPEARED FOR A DAY? WRITE YOUR IDEAS BELOW.

_____

_____

_____

_____

_____

_____

16.

PALEONTOLOGISTS WORK OUT WHAT EXTINCT ANIMALS LOOKED LIKE BY STUDYING FOSSILS. LOOK AT THIS FOSSILIZED FOOTPRINT, THEN DRAW WHAT YOU THINK THE ANIMAL LOOKED LIKE WHEN IT WAS ALIVE.

17.
IMAGINE YOU HAVE A ROBOT BEST FRIEND. DRAW THEM HERE. WHAT'S THEIR NAME?

18.
DID YOU KNOW THAT SOME ANIMALS CAN DO MATH? CROWS, MINNOWS, AND CHIMPANZEES HAVE ALL BEEN OBSERVED COUNTING! MAKE UP A REASON WHY AN ANIMAL MIGHT NEED TO COUNT.

19.
YOU MAKE AN AWARD-WINNING SCIENTIFIC DISCOVERY! DESCRIBE IT. IS IT A CURE? IS IT AN INVENTION?

20.

THERE ARE EIGHT PLANETS IN OUR SOLAR SYSTEM: MERCURY, VENUS, EARTH, MARS, JUPITER, SATURN, URANUS, AND NEPTUNE. IMAGINE A NEW PLANET SUDDENLY POPPED INTO EXISTENCE! DRAW IT BELOW, GIVE IT A NAME, THEN DESCRIBE IT. IS IT SCORCHING HOT, OR A WATERY WORLD? IS IT UNINHABITED, OR FULL OF LIFE?

21.

ALL SNOWFLAKES HAVE SIX IDENTICAL ARMS THAT ARE JOINED IN THE MIDDLE. THIS MEANS THEY HAVE ROTATIONAL AND REFLECTIONAL SYMMETRY—YOU CAN TURN ONE AROUND AND IT LOOKS THE SAME, AND YOU CAN DIVIDE IT IN HALF AND BOTH SIDES ARE EXACTLY THE SAME. FILL THIS SPACE WITH SNOWFLAKES.

22.

VIRUSES ARE EXTREMELY SMALL GERMS. THEY COME IN DIFFERENT SHAPES. IF YOU FOUND A NEW VIRUS, WHAT MIGHT IT LOOK LIKE? DRAW IT HERE.

23.

WHAT WORDS DO YOU THINK OF WHEN YOU READ THE WORD "TECHNOLOGY"? LIST THEM HERE.

24.

SCIENTISTS USED TO THINK THE ATOM WAS THE SMALLEST THING IN THE UNIVERSE—UNTIL THEY FOUND EVEN SMALLER PARTICLES INSIDE IT! YOU'RE A SCIENTIST AND YOU DISCOVER AN EVEN SMALLER PARTICLE— WHAT DO YOU CALL IT?

25.

A SPRING STORES ENERGY WHEN IT'S SQUASHED, WHICH IT RELEASES IN A SUDDEN JUMP WHEN LET GO. IMAGINE YOU'VE DESIGNED A PAIR OF SHOES WITH SPRINGS ON THE BOTTOM—WHAT DO YOU CALL THEM?

26.

ZOOLOGISTS ARE SCIENTISTS WHO STUDY ANIMALS. YOU'RE A ZOOLOGIST AND YOU'RE TRACKING A WILD ANIMAL. DRAW ITS FOOTPRINT.

27.

DO YOU KNOW WHY THE LEANING TOWER OF PISA IN ITALY LEANS? IT'S ALL BECAUSE OF A MISTAKE! THE BUILDERS CHOSE A SITE WHERE THE GROUND WAS TOO SOFT, CREATING AN UNSTEADY BASE FOR THE TOWER. DRAW A BUILDING, LIKE YOUR HOME, OR A FAMOUS LANDMARK, LIKE THE EIFFEL TOWER, BUT DRAW IT AS IF SOMETHING WENT WRONG DURING CONSTRUCTION!

28.

THE AIR ON EARTH HAS NO COLOR, SO IT'S INVISIBLE. WHAT WOULD IT BE LIKE ON A PLANET WITH GREEN AIR?

29.

AN OCTOPUS HAS SUCKERS ON ITS TENTACLES THAT IT USES TO HOLD THINGS. WHAT COULD YOU DO IF YOU HAD SUCKERS ON YOUR ARMS AND LEGS? WRITE FIVE IDEAS HERE.

1. _____

2. _____

3. _____

4. _____

5. _____

30.

A GEODE IS A SPECIAL KIND OF HOLLOW ROCK THAT HAS CRYSTALS GROWING INSIDE IT. DRAW CRYSTALS ON THE INSIDE SURFACE OF THIS GEODE.

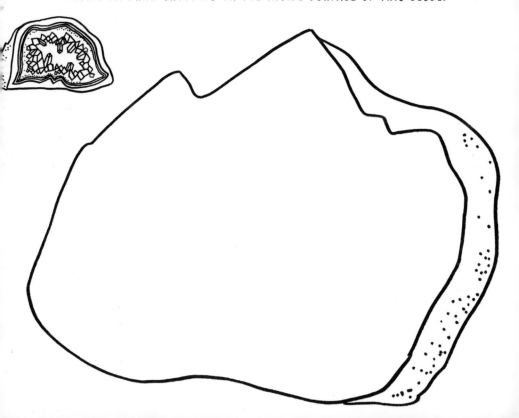

31.

IN ANCIENT TIMES, WHEN PEOPLE WANTED TO MEASURE THINGS, THEY OFTEN USED BODY PARTS AS THE "UNITS." FOR EXAMPLE, A "CUBIT" WAS THE DISTANCE BETWEEN ELBOW AND MIDDLE FINGERTIP IN ANCIENT EGYPT. MAKE UP A NEW UNIT OF MEASURE BASED ON WHATEVER YOU LIKE.

32.

SOME ANIMALS EAT ONLY ONE TYPE OF FOOD ALMOST ALL THE TIME: PANDAS EAT ONLY BAMBOO, AND KOALAS EAT ONLY EUCALYPTUS LEAVES. WHAT WOULD YOU EAT IF YOU HAD TO CHOOSE ONLY ONE FOOD?

33.

MUSICAL WIND INSTRUMENTS LIKE FLUTES AND TRUMPETS MAKE A SOUND BY BLOWING AIR THROUGH A TUBE. THE AIR VIBRATES, CAUSING THE SOUND. DRAW A DESIGN FOR A NEW WIND INSTRUMENT.

34.

DRONES ARE ROBOTS THAT CAN FLY TO HARD-TO-REACH PLACES. THEY CAN CARRY AND DELIVER OBJECTS, TAKE PICTURES, AND USE INFRARED SENSORS TO SEARCH FOR PEOPLE OR ANIMALS. DRAW SOMETHING FOR THIS DRONE TO CARRY. WHERE IS IT GOING?

35.

A PARACHUTE WORKS BY SLOWING DOWN THE PERSON OR OBJECT THAT'S FALLING. DRAW WHAT THIS PERSON CAN SEE WHILE THEY PARACHUTE TO EARTH.

36.

FOR A LONG TIME, MANY PEOPLE BELIEVED EARTH WAS FLAT! TODAY, WE KNOW IT'S A SPHERE. BUT IMAGINE OUR PLANET WAS ANOTHER SHAPE, LIKE A CUBE OR A SPIRAL! DRAW WHAT YOU IMAGINE HERE.

37.

SEA ANEMONES KEEP THEIR TENTACLES INSIDE THEIR BODIES WHEN RESTING OR IN A DRY PLACE. THEY THEN STRETCH THEM TO WAVE IN THE WATER TO CATCH FOOD INCLUDING SMALL FISH AND CRABS. DRAW MORE SEA ANEMONES AND SOMETHING FOR THEM TO EAT.

38.

DID YOU KNOW THAT HUMAN TEETH ARE AS STRONG AS SHARK TEETH? DRAW YOURSELF WITH A JAW FULL OF RAZOR-SHARP SHARK TEETH.

39.

A NEWLY HATCHED T. REX WAS ABOUT THREE FEET LONG—THE RIGHT SIZE FOR A PET! IMAGINE YOU HAD A PET BABY T. REX. WRITE A LETTER TO A FRIEND ABOUT WHAT IT'S LIKE.

40.

A MAGNIFYING GLASS IS A HANDY INVENTION—IT IS MADE UP OF A SPECIAL CURVED LENS THAT PRODUCES AN ENLARGED IMAGE. PEOPLE USE MAGNIFYING GLASSES TO SEE SMALL THINGS OR DETAILS MORE CLOSELY. DRAW WHAT YOU THINK THIS BUG WOULD LOOK LIKE THROUGH THE MAGNIFYING GLASS.

41.

SOME PLANTS AND ANIMALS ARE BRIGHTLY COLORED OR PATTERNED TO WARN PREDATORS THAT THEY ARE POISONOUS OR FOUL TASTING—THIS DEFENSE TACTIC IS CALLED APOSEMATISM. COLOR THESE PLANTS AND ANIMALS IN WARNING COLORS.

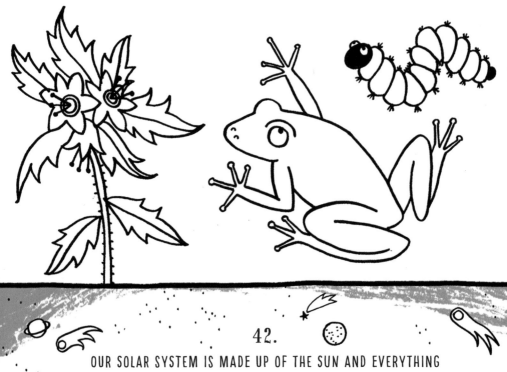

42.

OUR SOLAR SYSTEM IS MADE UP OF THE SUN AND EVERYTHING THAT REVOLVES AROUND IT, INCLUDING EIGHT PLANETS, THEIR MOONS, ASTEROIDS, METEORS, AND DWARF PLANETS. THERE ARE MANY SOLAR SYSTEMS IN THE UNIVERSE, MOST OF WHICH ARE UNKNOWN. DESIGN A NEW SOLAR SYSTEM HERE.

43.

IN A LAVA LAMP, WAX AT THE BOTTOM OF THE LAMP IS HEATED AND FLOATS TO THE TOP AS BLOBS. THE BLOBS THEN COOL AND SINK AGAIN. DRAW SOME COLORED BLOBS GOING UP AND DOWN IN THIS LAVA LAMP.

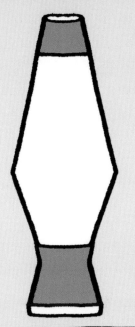

44.

ICEBERGS ARE HUGE CHUNKS OF ICE THAT BREAK OFF OF GLACIERS. IMAGINE YOU ARE AN ICEBERG BREAKING AWAY. HOW DO YOU FEEL ABOUT STRIKING OUT ON YOUR OWN?

45.

SCIENTISTS ARE TRYING TO MAKE A NEW KIND OF DINOSAUR BY CHANGING THE GENES OF A CHICKEN. IF YOU COULD CHOOSE A MODERN-DAY ANIMAL OTHER THAN A CHICKEN TO MAKE A DINOSAUR, WHAT WOULD YOU CHOOSE?

46.

BY BENDING MIRRORS, WE CAN MAKE WIGGLY, DISTORTED REFLECTIONS.
DRAW YOURSELF WIGGLY AND WONKY ON THIS MIRROR.

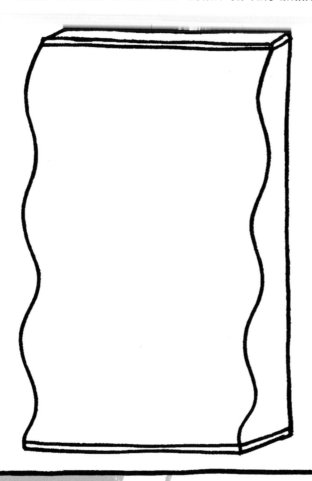

47.

MARS HAS TWO MOONS. IF EARTH HAD AN EXTRA MOON, WHAT WOULD YOU CALL IT?

48.

CUTTLEFISH COMMUNICATE WITH EACH OTHER BY FLASHING DIFFERENT COLORS OVER THEIR SKIN. DRAW BRIGHT PATTERNS ON THESE CUTTLEFISH AND WRITE WHAT THEY ARE SAYING WITH THEIR COLORS IN THE SPEECH BUBBLES.

49.

A ROBOT FLOOR CLEANER HAS SENSORS INSIDE IT THAT HELP IT TO AVOID THINGS IN ITS WAY, LIKE FURNITURE AND DROPPED TOYS. DRAW SOME THINGS FOR THIS ROBOT CLEANER TO AVOID, AND A PATH IT COULD TAKE OVER THE FLOOR.

50.

DID YOU KNOW THAT POTATOES CAN PRODUCE ELECTRICITY? IF YOU STICK A ZINC NAIL AND A COPPER COIN INTO A POTATO AND ATTACH WIRES TO THEM, YOU CAN MAKE A POTATO BATTERY! DRAW SOMETHING FOR THIS POTATO BATTERY TO POWER.

51.

IMAGINE YOU'RE A SCIENTIST WHO HAS DISCOVERED HOW TO SHRINK THINGS AND YOU'VE ACCIDENTALLY SHRUNK YOURSELF DOWN TO THE SIZE OF AN ANT! WHAT HAPPENS NEXT?

52.

KOALAS HAVE FINGERPRINTS, JUST LIKE US! DRAW FINGERPRINTS ON THIS KOALA HAND.

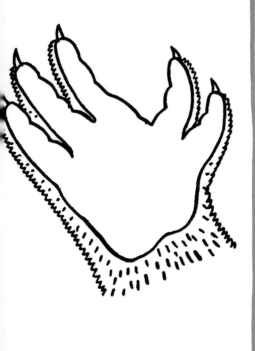

53.

THE MARS LANDER INSIGHT IS A NASA ROBOT THAT WAS SENT TO MARS TO STUDY THE PLANET. ONE OF ITS FINDINGS IS A STRANGE "HUMMING" SOUND. NO ONE KNOWS WHAT IT IS! WHAT DO YOU THINK MIGHT BE CAUSING IT? WRITE YOUR THEORY HERE.

_____

_____

_____

_____

_____

_____

_____

54.

LITTLE BROWN BATS CAN SLEEP FOR UP TO 19 HOURS A DAY, WHILE GIRAFFES CAN SLEEP FOR LESS THAN 1 HOUR A DAY! WHICH WOULD YOU RATHER DO, AND WHY?

55.

DID YOU KNOW THAT STARDUST IS REAL? IT'S MADE UP OF BITS OF ANCIENT STARS, AND IT HAS BEEN FOUND ON METEORITES THAT HAVE LANDED ON EARTH. FILL THIS VIAL WITH DRAWINGS OF STARDUST— WHAT COLORS WILL YOU USE?

56.

PARALLEL LINES STAY THE SAME DISTANCE APART FOREVER AND NEVER MEET. TURN THESE PARALLEL LINES INTO A DRAWING OF SOMETHING.

57.

SWISS ENGINEER GEORGE DE MESTRAL INVENTED VELCRO AFTER PICKING STICKY BURRS FROM HIS DOG MILKA'S FUR! HE SAW HOW THE BURRS HAD HUNDREDS OF TINY "HOOKS" THAT ATTACHED TO FUR AND CLOTHING. CAN YOU THINK OF SOMETHING IN NATURE THAT COULD INSPIRE A NEW INVENTION?

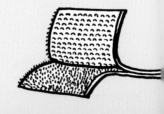

58.

SOUND WAVES CAN BE REFLECTED BACK—THIS IS CALLED AN ECHO. ECHOES CAN BE HEARD IN ENCLOSED SPACES OR SPACES WHERE THERE ARE LOTS OF HARD SURFACES. WHAT WOULD YOU SHOUT INTO A CAVE TO HEAR ECHOED? WRITE IT INSIDE THE CAVE.

59.

TODAY, WE KNOW THAT EARTH'S CORE IS MADE OF METAL (LIQUID AND SOLID), BUT PEOPLE USED TO THINK EARTH WAS HOLLOW. MAKE UP YOUR OWN WILD THEORY ABOUT WHAT'S INSIDE EARTH.

60.

SOME ANIMALS SPEND MUCH OF THEIR LIVES UPSIDE DOWN, SUCH AS BATS. INVENT A NEW TYPE OF ANIMAL THAT LIVES UPSIDE DOWN. WHAT IS IT CALLED? DESCRIBE IT.

61.

LASERS PRODUCE VERY NARROW BEAMS OF LIGHT CONTAINING A LOT OF ENERGY. THEY CAN BE USED TO CUT THROUGH MATERIALS. DESIGN A NEW INVENTION THAT FIRES LASER BEAMS.

62.

INSECTS ARE A GROUP OF ANIMALS THAT HAVE A HARD OUTER SKELETON, THREE-PART BODIES, SIX LEGS, AND TWO ANTENNAE—MANY ALSO HAVE WINGS. LIST AS MANY INSECTS AS YOU CAN THINK OF.

63.

A SQUARE IS A TYPE OF RECTANGLE WHERE ALL SIDES ARE THE SAME LENGTH. USE A RULER AND PENCIL TO FILL THIS RECTANGLE WITH LOTS OF TINY SQUARES.

64.

IMAGINE YOU INVENTED A NEW TYPE OF METAL THAT WAS AS BENDY AS GELATIN BUT SUPERSTRONG. WHAT WOULD YOU USE IT FOR?

_____

_____

_____

_____

_____

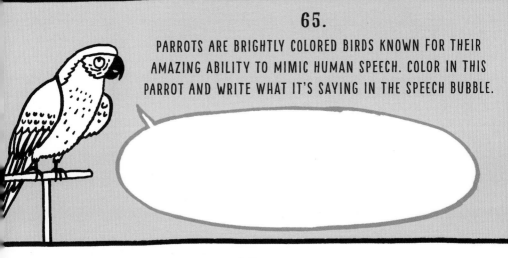

65.

PARROTS ARE BRIGHTLY COLORED BIRDS KNOWN FOR THEIR AMAZING ABILITY TO MIMIC HUMAN SPEECH. COLOR IN THIS PARROT AND WRITE WHAT IT'S SAYING IN THE SPEECH BUBBLE.

66.

WHEN PEOPLE INVENTED MICROSCOPES MORE THAN 400 YEARS AGO, THEY RUSHED TO LOOK AT ALL KINDS OF THINGS INCLUDING SALIVA, POND WATER, AND THE LEAVES OF PLANTS. WHAT WOULD YOU LIKE TO LOOK AT UNDER A MICROSCOPE?

67.

ARTIFICIAL REEFS ARE MAN-MADE STRUCTURES PLACED OR LEFT IN THE OCEAN. THEY CAN ENCOURAGE MARINE LIFE, SINCE CORALS, BARNACLES, AND ALGAE OFTEN ATTACH THEMSELVES TO THE STRUCTURES, AND OTHER MARINE ANIMALS ARRIVE TO FEED ON THEM. TURN THIS SHIPWRECK INTO AN ARTIFICIAL REEF BUSTLING WITH ALL KINDS OF MARINE CREATURES.

68.

BEFORE MODERN MEDICINE, PEOPLE USED SOME VERY ODD TREATMENTS FOR ILLNESSES. ANCIENT EGYPTIANS OFTEN USED ANIMAL DUNG, VARIOUS PLANTS, BLOOD, AND EVEN HUMAN BRAINS TO CURE THEIR ILLS! MAKE UP A RECIPE TO CURE A COMMON COLD USING STRANGE OR GROSS INGREDIENTS.

69.

BRITISH SCIENTIST JANE GOODALL IS FAMOUS FOR STUDYING CHIMPANZEES IN THE WILD. SHE GAVE THEM NAMES—HER FAVORITE WAS CALLED DAVID GREYBEARD. NAME THIS CHIMP.

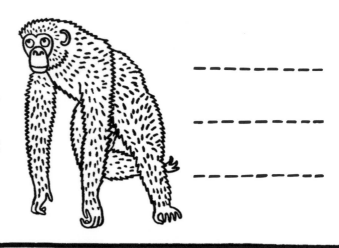

_ _ _ _ _ _ _ _ _

_ _ _ _ _ _ _ _ _

_ _ _ _ _ _ _ _ _

70.

A TOTAL SOLAR ECLIPSE HAPPENS WHEN THE MOON ENTIRELY BLOCKS OUT THE SUN IN THE SKY FOR A FEW MINUTES. DESCRIBE WHAT IT MIGHT BE LIKE TO SEE A TOTAL SOLAR ECLIPSE. WOULD YOU FEEL AFRAID OR EXCITED?

71.

A PIECE OF GOLD THE SIZE OF A SMALL COIN, WEIGHING JUST 1 OUNCE, CAN BE HAMMERED INTO A SHEET SO THIN IT WOULD COVER 100 SQUARE FEET—ROUGHLY ENOUGH TO COVER TEN 55-POUND CHILDREN! IF YOU COULD COVER ANYTHING IN GOLD, WHAT WOULD YOU CHOOSE?

72.

A GOLF CLUB HAS A SMALL HEAD FOR HITTING A BALL A LONG WAY, WHILE A
TENNIS RACKET HAS A LARGE AREA AND HITS A BALL A SHORTER DISTANCE.
DESIGN A NEW KIND OF CLUB OR BAT. WHAT GAME WOULD YOU PLAY WITH IT?

73.

ELECTRIC DEVICES OFTEN MAKE LIFE EASIER OR NICER.
LIST THE FIRST FOUR HELPFUL ELECTRIC DEVICES YOU CAN THINK OF.

1. _____
2. _____
3. _____
4. _____

74.

TREES IN A FOREST ARE LINKED BY NETWORKS OF
UNDERGROUND ROOTS, FUNGI, AND BACTERIA THAT
THEY USE TO SHARE FOOD AND MINERALS. CONNECT
THE UNDERGROUND NETWORK BETWEEN THE TREES.

75.

ASTRONOMERS ARE SCIENTISTS WHO STUDY THE UNIVERSE. THEY OFTEN USE HIGH-POWERED TELESCOPES TO STUDY THE STARS AND PLANETS. DRAW SOMETHING INSIDE THE TELESCOPE LENS.

76.

INVISIBLE INK LETS YOU DRAW OR WRITE SOMETHING THAT DOESN'T SHOW UP ON PAPER UNTIL IT'S HEATED OR PUT UNDER A SPECIAL TYPE OF LIGHT. WRITE A MESSAGE THAT YOU WOULD SEND IN INVISIBLE INK.

TOP SECRET

77.
DESIGN A BUILDING ... MADE ENTIRELY
OF TRIANGLES!

78.
THE NUMBERS WE USE TODAY ARE
DEVELOPED FROM ANCIENT HINDU-
ARABIC NUMBERS USED MORE THAN
1,000 YEARS AGO. CAN YOU INVENT
NEW SYMBOLS TO REPLACE THEM?

$0 \rightarrow$

$1 \rightarrow$

$2 \rightarrow$

$3 \rightarrow$

$4 \rightarrow$

$5 \rightarrow$

$6 \rightarrow$

$7 \rightarrow$

$8 \rightarrow$

$9 \rightarrow$

79.
A SINGLE RAIN CLOUD CAN CONTAIN ABOUT 550 TONS OF WATER.
THAT'S AS HEAVY AS ABOUT 80 AFRICAN BUSH ELEPHANTS!
DRAW AN ELEPHANT-SHAPED CLOUD HERE.

80.

SCIENTISTS CARRY OUT EXPERIMENTS TO FIND THE ANSWERS TO QUESTIONS. WHICH QUESTION WOULD YOU MOST LIKE SCIENTISTS TO ANSWER?

_____

_____

_____

81.

THE WHEEL HAS MADE MOVING AND TRANSPORTING THINGS MUCH EASIER. ADD TO THIS WHEEL TO MAKE A NEW INVENTION OR MACHINE.

82.

DIFFERENT TREES HAVE DIFFERENT SHAPED LEAVES. TRACHYANDRA PLANTS THAT GROW IN EASTERN AND SOUTHERN AFRICA HAVE CURLY LEAVES LIKE CORKSCREWS. FILL THIS SPACE WITH REALLY STRANGE LEAVES.

83.

PUMICE IS A TYPE OF ROCK WITH LOTS OF TINY HOLES IN IT. IT IS FORMED DURING VOLCANIC ERUPTIONS WHEN GASES IN THE LAVA ESCAPE AS THE LAVA COOLS. IT'S SO LIGHT IT CAN FLOAT ON WATER! WHAT WOULD YOU MAKE FROM PUMICE?

84.

A MAGNET ATTRACTS THINGS MADE OF IRON OR STEEL. DRAW OR LIST SOME THINGS THAT WOULD STICK TO THIS MAGNET.

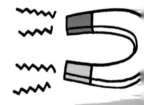

85.

AN X-RAY SHOWS THE BONES INSIDE A BODY. DRAW SOME BONES IN THIS BOX TO MAKE AN X-RAY PICTURE. COLOR THE BONES WHITE AND THE BACKGROUND BLACK.

86.

LONG AGO, ALL THE LAND ON EARTH WAS JOINED IN ONE "SUPERCONTINENT," CALLED PANGAEA. OVER TIME, THE LAND SHIFTED AND BROKE APART. IMAGINE THAT ALL THE CONTINENTS JOINED UP AGAIN INTO A NEW CONTINENT! DRAW IT BELOW AND GIVE IT A NAME.

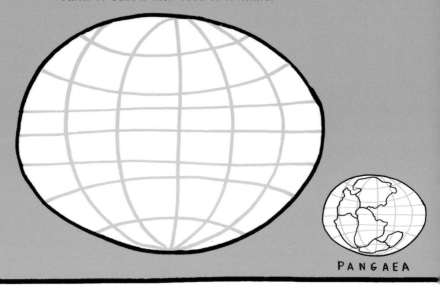

PANGAEA

87.

MANY GREEN LEAVES CHANGE COLOR IN THE FALL BECAUSE THE REDUCTION IN SUNLIGHT CAUSES THE CHEMICAL THAT MAKES THEM GREEN TO BREAK DOWN, LEAVING ONLY THE YELLOW, RED, ORANGE, AND BROWN PIGMENTS. COLOR THESE LEAVES IN FALL SHADES.

88.

GALAXIES ARE HUGE COLLECTIONS OF BILLIONS OF STARS AND THEIR SOLAR SYSTEMS. FROM FAR AWAY, THEY LOOK LIKE SMUDGES OF LIGHT. MOST GALAXIES ARE SHAPED LIKE SPIRALS, INCLUDING OUR GALAXY—THE MILKY WAY. FILL THIS SPACE WITH MORE DRAWINGS OF SPIRAL GALAXIES. GIVE THEM NAMES, TOO!

THE MILKY WAY

89.

A SAILBOAT IS DRIVEN ALONG BY WIND PUSHING AGAINST THE SAILS. ADD SAILS TO THIS BOAT AND DECORATE THEM.

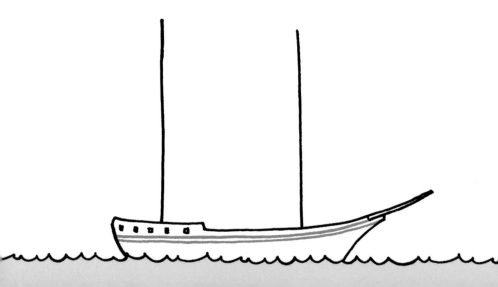

90.

MANY ANIMALS ARE CAMOUFLAGED—
THEY HAVE A PATTERN ON THEIR SKIN,
FUR, OR FEATHERS THAT HELPS THEM TO
BLEND INTO THE BACKGROUND, HIDING
THEM FROM PREDATORS. IMAGINE WE
HAD THE POWER TO CAMOUFLAGE OUR
SKIN! COLOR THIS HAND TO BLEND IN
WITH A LEAFY FOREST.

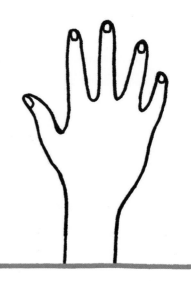

91.

SCIENTISTS OFTEN MAKE PERFUMES BY USING NATURAL OILS FROM PLANTS
SUCH AS ROSES AND LEMONS. DESCRIBE YOUR DREAM PERFUME—WOULD IT
SMELL LIKE A FLOWER YOU LOVE? OR A FAVORITE FOOD?

92.

WHEN CANNED FOOD WAS FIRST INVENTED, THERE WERE NO CAN OPENERS.
HOW DO YOU THINK PEOPLE OPENED THE CANS? WRITE THREE IDEAS HERE.

1. _____

2. _____

3. _____

93.

IN THE EARLY DAYS OF SPACE TRAVEL ASTRONAUTS TOOK FREEZE-DRIED FOODS INTO SPACE. FREEZE-DRYING IS A SPECIAL PROCESS THAT REMOVES ALL MOISTURE, MAKING THE FOOD EASIER TO PRESERVE AND STORE. WHAT WOULD YOU PUT ON YOUR SPACE MENU?

94.

SOME ANTS CAN CARRY OBJECTS MANY TIMES THEIR OWN SIZE. DRAW A TOWER OF UNEXPECTED OBJECTS FOR THIS ANT TO CARRY.

95.

HOW DO YOU THINK HUMANS WILL BE TRAVELING AROUND IN THE YEAR 2100? DRAW OR DESCRIBE A TYPE OF VEHICLE YOU THINK WE MIGHT HAVE THEN.

96.

IMAGINE YOU'RE A BOTANIST—A SCIENTIST WHO STUDIES PLANTS—AND YOU'VE FOUND A NEW PLANT. WHAT WILL YOU CALL IT? DRAW IT HERE, LABELING THE STEM, LEAVES, ROOTS, AND ANY FLOWERS OR FRUIT IT HAS.

97.

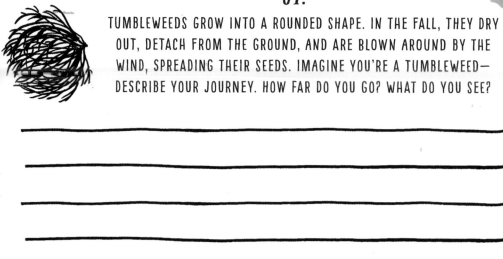

TUMBLEWEEDS GROW INTO A ROUNDED SHAPE. IN THE FALL, THEY DRY OUT, DETACH FROM THE GROUND, AND ARE BLOWN AROUND BY THE WIND, SPREADING THEIR SEEDS. IMAGINE YOU'RE A TUMBLEWEED— DESCRIBE YOUR JOURNEY. HOW FAR DO YOU GO? WHAT DO YOU SEE?

98.

SCIENTISTS ARE WORKING ON AN "INVISIBILITY CLOAK" THAT BENDS LIGHT AROUND AN OBJECT TO SHOW WHAT'S BEHIND IT. WHAT WOULD YOU DO IF YOU HAD AN INVISIBILITY CLOAK? WRITE SOME IDEAS HERE.

99.

A MIRROR SHOWS A REFLECTION OF AN OBJECT SO THAT IT'S THE OTHER WAY AROUND. DRAW THE REFLECTION OF THIS FACE IN THE MIRROR. USE THE EXAMPLE TO HELP YOU.

EXAMPLE

100.

YOU'RE ASKED TO WRITE A SHORT MESSAGE THAT WILL BE LAUNCHED INTO SPACE FOR POTENTIAL ALIENS TO SEE. WHAT WOULD IT SAY?

101. MUSHROOMS AND TOADSTOOLS GROW UP FROM THE GROUND, OR ON WOOD OR OTHER SURFACES. DRAW SOME COLORFUL MUSHROOMS ON THIS LOG.

102. ICE IS FROZEN WATER. AS SOON AS IT'S ABOVE FREEZING, IT STARTS TO MELT. WHAT WOULD YOU MAKE FROM ICE THAT YOU COULD USE FOR A WHILE AND WOULD THEN MELT AWAY?

_____

_____

_____

_____

103. YOU CAN ATTACH A DYNAMO (ELECTRICAL GENERATOR) TO A BICYCLE SO THAT IT GENERATES ELECTRICITY AS YOU CYCLE, WHICH CAN THEN BE USED TO POWER THE BIKE'S LIGHTS. WHAT WOULD YOU USE THE ELECTRICITY FOR IF YOU HAD A DYNAMO ON YOUR RUNNING SHOES?

104. A HOVERCRAFT FLOATS ON A CUSHION OF AIR OVER THE GROUND OR WATER. DRAW A HOVERCRAFT OF YOUR OWN—IT COULD BE A CHAIR HOVERCRAFT, A BED HOVERCRAFT, OR WHATEVER YOU LIKE!

105. BEFORE THE DINOSAURS, THERE WERE DRAGONFLIES THE SIZE OF PIGEONS! WRITE A STORY ABOUT FINDING A GIANT INSECT.

106.

FIRE USUALLY BURNS WITH A YELLOW-ORANGE FLAME, BUT SOME METALS MAKE DIFFERENT COLORED FLAMES—DEEP RED, MAUVE, EVEN GREEN! COLOR THESE FLAMES IN DIFFERENT COLORS.

107.

IT'S SAID THAT ENGLISH SCIENTIST ISAAC NEWTON CAME UP WITH HIS THEORY OF GRAVITY AFTER AN APPLE FELL ON HIS HEAD. IT'S QUITE POSSIBLY NOT TRUE—BUT DRAW THE APPLE ANYWAY!

108.

WHAT'S YOUR FAVORITE INVENTION OF ALL TIME? WHY IS IT YOUR FAVORITE?

_____

_____

_____

_____

109.

HAILSTONES ARE LUMPS OF ICE THAT FORM IN THUNDERCLOUDS DURING COLD, WET WEATHER. WHEN THE LUMPS GET TOO LARGE, THEY FALL TO THE GROUND. THE LARGEST-KNOWN HAILSTONE WAS 8 INCHES ACROSS! WRITE A SHORT POEM ABOUT A STORM OF GIANT HAILSTONES.

_____

_____

_____

_____

_____

_____

_____

_____

_____

_____

110.

A DIAGONAL LINE CUTS A SQUARE INTO TWO TRIANGLES. YOU CAN SPLIT THE TRIANGLES INTO MORE AND MORE TRIANGLES. LOOK AT THE EXAMPLE, THEN MAKE YOUR OWN PATTERN OF TRIANGLES IN THE EMPTY SQUARE.

EXAMPLE

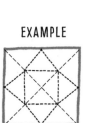

111.

COMPUTER PROGRAMS TELL A COMPUTER EXACTLY WHAT TO DO. THEY CAN'T MISS ANY STEPS IN THE INSTRUCTIONS! WRITE INSTRUCTIONS FOR BRUSHING YOUR TEETH THAT A ROBOT COULD FOLLOW.

_____

_____

_____

_____

_____

_____

_____

112.

A WILL-O'-THE WISP IS A BLUE FLAME SEEN OVER BOGS AND SWAMPS. IT'S MADE BY MARSH GAS ESCAPING AND BURNING, BUT PEOPLE ONCE THOUGHT IT WAS A SPIRIT OR GHOST! DRAW SOME WILL-O'-THE-WISPS ON THE SURFACE OF THIS BOG.

113.

A ROCKET WORKS BY BURNING A LOT OF FUEL QUICKLY IN A SMALL SPACE. IT MAKES A LOT OF HOT GAS THAT RUSHES OUT OF THE BACK OF THE ROCKET, FORCING IT FORWARD. DRAW A FIERY BLAST RUSHING OUT OF THIS ROCKET.

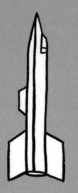

114.

SPIDER SILK IS INCREDIBLY STRONG FOR ITS WEIGHT. DRAW SOMETHING HEAVY DANGLING FROM THIS THREAD OF SPIDER SILK.

115.

CONNECT THE DOTTED LINES TO TURN THIS SQUARE INTO A CUBE. THEN FILL THE SPACE WITH DRAWINGS OF MORE CUBES.

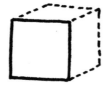

116.

COMETS ARE CHUNKS OF FROZEN GASES, ROCK, AND DUST THAT ORBIT THE SUN. AS A COMET GETS CLOSER TO THE SUN, IT HEATS UP, FORMING A GLOWING HEAD WITH A TAIL OF GAS AND DUST THAT STRETCHES FOR MILLIONS OF MILES! DRAW SOME COMETS AROUND THE SUN—THE TAILS ALWAYS POINT AWAY FROM THE SUN.

117.

SOME VEHICLES USE CATERPILLAR TRACKS, WHICH ARE MADE UP OF MANY WHEELS INSIDE A WIDE BAND TURNED BY THE WHEELS. THIS HELPS VEHICLES TRAVEL OVER UNEVEN GROUND. DRAW YOUR OWN VEHICLE ON THESE CATERPILLAR TRACKS. WHERE WOULD YOU TAKE IT?

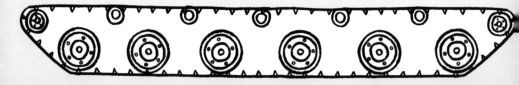

118.

SCIENTIST BENJAMIN FRANKLIN FAMOUSLY USED A KITE TO SHOW THAT LIGHTNING IS ELECTRICITY IN THE SKY. DESIGN A NEW KITE FOR FRANKLIN TO USE.

119.

DESIGN SOME SPECIAL SHOES ... FOR WALKING ON WATER!

120.

YOU FIND THIS TOOTH ON THE BEACH. DRAW THE KIND OF CREATURE YOU THINK IT MIGHT HAVE COME FROM.

121.

IMAGINE YOU HAVE MADE AN INFLATABLE BICYCLE. LIST THREE GOOD THINGS AND THREE BAD THINGS ABOUT YOUR INVENTION.

GOOD THINGS:

1.

_____

2.

_____

3.

_____

BAD THINGS:

1.

_____

2.

_____

3.

_____

122.

AROUND THE WORLD YOU CAN FIND STATUES OF BRILLIANT SCIENTISTS, HONORING AND REMEMBERING THEIR WORK. IF YOU COULD HAVE A STATUE OF A SCIENTIST IN YOUR HOMETOWN, WHO WOULD YOU CHOOSE? DRAW A STATUE OF THEM AND WRITE THEIR NAME.

123. A FACE MASK CAN HELP STOP THE SPREAD OF DISEASES PASSED ON THROUGH OUR BREATH. DECORATE AN EXCITING-LOOKING FACE MASK FOR YOURSELF.

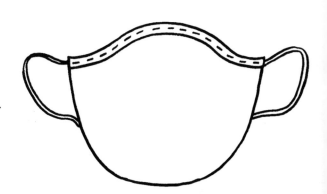

124. WORMS MAY NOT SEEM VERY SPECIAL, BUT THEY DO IMPORTANT WORK— BREAKING DOWN PLANT MATTER, EVENTUALLY MAKING NEW SOIL. DRAW SOME WORMS AT WORK IN THE SOIL UNDER THIS FOREST FLOOR.

125. A CAMERA TAKES A STILL PHOTO; A VIDEO CAMERA RECORDS A MOVING IMAGE AND SOUND. WHAT WOULD YOU LIKE THE NEXT INVENTION TO BE TO HELP YOU RECORD AND SHARE MEMORIES?

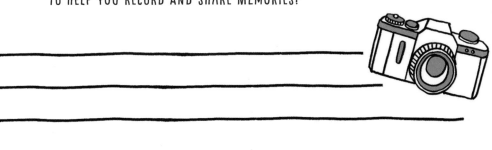

126.

THE HORNS OF ANIMALS SUCH AS RHINOS ARE MADE OF THE SAME MATERIAL AS YOUR FINGERNAILS AND HAIR, CALLED KERATIN. WHAT WOULD YOU LOOK LIKE WITH HORNS? DRAW YOURSELF HERE WITH ONE OR MORE HORNS.

127.

REWILDING IS LETTING PLANTS AND ANIMALS RETURN TO AN AREA THAT HAS BEEN USED BY HUMANS. IT'S A WAY OF HELPING THE NATURAL WORLD RECOVER. REWILD THIS FIELD WITH PLANTS AND ANIMALS.

128.

THE FIRST LONG-DISTANCE CAR TRIP WAS MADE BY BERTHA BENZ, WHO DROVE 65 MILES ACROSS GERMANY. IF YOU HAD TO TAKE A VEHICLE ON ITS FIRST TEST DRIVE, WHERE WOULD YOU LIKE TO GO?

129.

THERMOSES KEEP LIQUIDS INSIDE THEM AT STEADY TEMPERATURES. DECORATE THIS THERMOS, THEN WRITE WHAT DRINK YOU WOULD KEEP INSIDE IT.

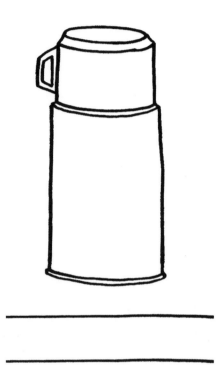

130.

DID YOU KNOW THAT ALL MAMMALS HAVE HAIR? EVEN DOLPHINS! DOLPHINS ARE BORN WITH HAIR AROUND THEIR JAWS WHICH USUALLY FALLS OUT AS THEY GET OLDER. ADD SOME HAIR TO THIS DOLPHIN.

131.

ENCELADUS IS THE NAME OF ONE OF SATURN'S MOONS. ITS SURFACE HAS A LAYER OF ICE UP TO 16 MILES THICK! WHAT DO YOU THINK MIGHT BE UNDER THE ICE?

_____

_____

_____

132.

THE METAL COBALT IS NAMED AFTER A TYPE OF MISCHIEVOUS GOBLIN FROM GERMAN FOLKLORE CALLED A "KOBOLD." MEDIEVAL MINERS THOUGHT THE METAL WAS HARMFUL AND TROUBLESOME, JUST LIKE THE GOBLINS! DRAW WHAT YOU THINK A KOBOLD LOOKED LIKE.

133.

DECORATOR CRABS STICK THINGS ON THEIR SHELLS, OFTEN ADDING DANGEROUS ANIMALS AND POISONOUS PLANTS AS PROTECTION AGAINST ANYTHING THAT MIGHT WANT TO EAT THEM. DECORATE THIS CRAB IN ANY WAY YOU LIKE.

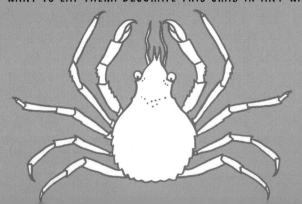

134.

FOG IS MADE OF DROPLETS OF WATER HANGING IN THE AIR NEAR THE GROUND—LIKE A CLOUD THAT HAS FALLEN DOWN! IT'S HARD TO SEE THROUGH FOG. WRITE A SHORT STORY ABOUT SOMETHING THAT HAPPENS ON A WALK IN THE FOG.

135.

MACHINES ARE OFTEN USED TO HELP US PERFORM TASKS; THEY MAKE THINGS EASIER. INVENT A MACHINE THAT SERVES NO PURPOSE AND DOESN'T HELP AT ALL!

136.

AMMONITES WERE SQUID-LIKE MARINE ANIMALS THAT LIVED IN CURLED SHELLS. THEY LIVED AROUND THE SAME TIME AS SOME DINOSAURS. DRAW SOME MORE AMMONITES HERE.

137.

BECAUSE OF DIFFERENCES IN GRAVITY AND ATMOSPHERE, YOU COULD THROW A BALL THREE TIMES AS FAR ON MARS AS ON EARTH. DRAW SOME ALIENS PLAYING CATCH ON MARS.

138.

RIVERS RARELY RUN IN A STRAIGHT LINE; THEY FLOW DOWN SLOPES, BEND AROUND BUMPS IN THE LAND, AND FALL OVER ROCKS. DRAW A WINDING RIVER IN THIS SPACE.

140.

A DANDELION USES THE WIND TO CARRY ITS SEEDS. WITH A PUFF OF THE BREEZE, THEY ALL FLOAT AWAY. DRAW THE REST OF THE SEEDS COMING FROM THIS DANDELION HEAD.

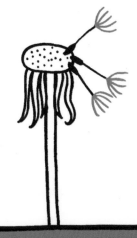

139.

SODA CONTAINS CARBON DIOXIDE, WHICH ESCAPES AS BUBBLES. IF YOU SHAKE THE DRINK BEFORE YOU OPEN IT, LOTS MORE BUBBLES FORM, MAKING THE GAS ESCAPE QUICKER AND RESULTING IN MORE FIZZ! DRAW A FIZZ EXPLOSION COMING FROM THIS OPEN BOTTLE.

141.

GLASSES HELP PEOPLE SEE, AND HEARING AIDS HELP THEM HEAR. WHAT DO YOU THINK A DEVICE TO HELP PEOPLE SMELL MIGHT LOOK LIKE? DRAW IT HERE.

142.

THE VISORS ON SPACE SUITS ARE COVERED WITH A VERY THIN LAYER OF GOLD FOR PROTECTION FROM SUNLIGHT. THE OUTSIDE WORKS A BIT LIKE A MIRROR. DRAW A REFLECTION IN THIS ASTRONAUT'S VISOR, SHOWING WHAT THEY CAN SEE.

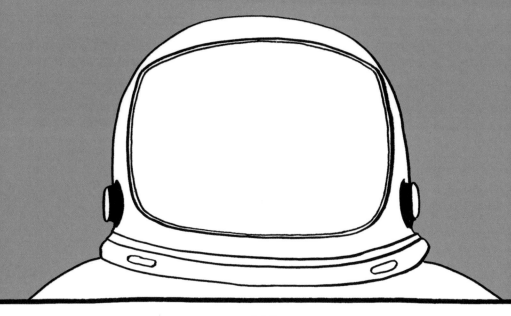

143.

A CLONE IS AN EXACT COPY OF A PLANT OR ANIMAL. WRITE A SHORT STORY ABOUT WHAT YOU WOULD DO IF YOU COULD MAKE A CLONE OF YOURSELF.

144.

SOME ANIMALS ARE HERBIVORES—THEY EAT PLANTS. OTHERS ARE CARNIVORES—THEY EAT OTHER ANIMALS. HERBIVORES HAVE AN EASIER TIME FINDING FOOD, BUT THEY HAVE TO BEWARE OF CARNIVORES! WHICH WOULD YOU RATHER BE?

145.

STRINGED INSTRUMENTS SUCH AS GUITARS OR VIOLINS MAKE A SOUND WHEN THEIR STRINGS VIBRATE IN THE AIR. DESIGN A NEW TYPE OF STRINGED INSTRUMENT.

146.

BIRDS HAVE FEATHERS TO KEEP WARM, BEARS HAVE FUR, AND SEALS HAVE A THICK LAYER OF FAT. WHICH TYPE OF INSULATION WOULD YOU RATHER HAVE? WHY?

147.

ANIMALS IN TIDE POOLS HAVE WATER FLOODING INTO THEIR HOME TWICE A DAY. IF THEY ARE NOT ATTACHED TO A ROCK, THEY CAN GET WASHED AWAY. IMAGINE YOU LIVED IN A TIDE POOL. WHAT WOULD IT BE LIKE AS THE TIDE COMES IN? EXCITING OR SCARY? WRITE ABOUT IT HERE.

148.

BLACK HOLES ARE AREAS OF EXTREME GRAVITY IN SPACE THAT CAN DRAW IN ANYTHING THAT STRAYS TOO NEAR AND DESTROY IT. DESIGN A SIGN TO WARN SPACESHIPS OF NEARBY BLACK HOLES.

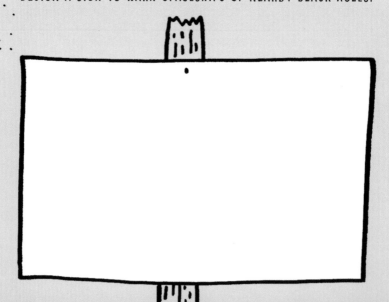

149.

ICE POPS WERE INVENTED ACCIDENTALLY BY AN 11-YEAR-OLD BOY. HE MIXED SODA POWDER AND WATER AND LEFT IT OUTSIDE OVERNIGHT WITH A STICK IN IT, AND IT FROZE SOLID. THINK OF YOUR FAVORITE FOOD, THEN MAKE UP A STORY ABOUT HOW IT WAS INVENTED.

_____

_____

_____

_____

_____

_____

150.

EPIPHYTES ARE PLANTS THAT GROW ON TREES. THEY RELY ON THE TREES FOR PHYSICAL SUPPORT BUT THEY DON'T HARM THEM. DRAW MORE EPIPHYTES ON THIS TREE.

151.

A CONE HAS A CIRCLE AT THE BASE AND SIDES THAT REACH A POINT. DRAW A PICTURE THAT INCLUDES THIS CONE.

152.

SEA SLUGS COME IN ALL KINDS OF COLORS, WITH FRILLS AND BITS THAT STICK OUT IN ODD PLACES. IT'S THOUGHT THAT THEIR BRIGHT COLORS HELP SCARE OFF PREDATORS. INVENT YOUR OWN THEORY ABOUT WHY SEA SLUGS LOOK THE WAY THEY DO.

_ _ _ _ _ _ _ _ _ _ _

_ _ _ _ _ _ _ _ _ _ _

_ _ _ _ _ _ _ _ _ _ _

_ _ _ _ _ _ _ _ _

153.

A PERISCOPE USES AN ARRANGEMENT OF MIRRORS IN A TUBE TO ALLOW YOU TO SEE OVER AND AROUND OBJECTS AND OBSTACLES. SUBMARINES USED TO USE PERISCOPES TO SHOW WHAT WAS HAPPENING AT THE OCEAN'S SURFACE. WHAT WOULD YOU USE A PERISCOPE FOR?

154.

DIFFERENT MATERIALS HAVE DIFFERENT PHYSICAL PROPERTIES THAT WE CAN USE TO DESCRIBE HOW THEY LOOK AND FEEL. FOR EACH OF THE PROPERTIES LISTED BELOW, FIND AN ITEM IN YOUR HOME WITH THAT PROPERTY.

HARD: _____

SQUASHY: _____

ABSORBENT (SOAKS UP WATER): _____

MALLEABLE (CAN BE BENT): _____

STICKY: _____

TRANSLUCENT (SEE-THROUGH): _____

ELASTIC (CAN BE STRETCHED AND THEN RETURN TO ITS ORIGINAL SHAPE): _____

_____

155.

DURING THE STONE AGE, PEOPLE PAINTED ANIMALS ON THE WALLS OF THEIR CAVES. SCIENTISTS CAN LEARN ABOUT THE ANIMALS THAT LIVED AT THAT TIME FROM THESE PICTURES. DRAW SOME MODERN-DAY ANIMALS ON THIS CAVE WALL.

156.

MARINE SCIENTISTS STUDYING SHARKS SOMETIMES DIVE USING A CAGE TO KEEP THEMSELVES SAFE. DRAW A CAGE AROUND THIS DIVER TO PROTECT HER.

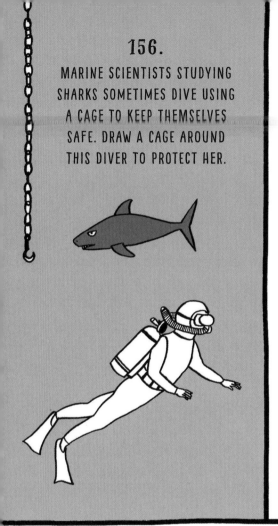

157.

TO CAMOUFLAGE THEMSELVES, AUSTRALIAN WRAP-AROUND SPIDERS CAN FLATTEN THEIR BODIES AND WRAP THEMSELVES AROUND A BRANCH LIKE A BANDAGE! IF YOU COULD MAKE YOUR BODY GO FLAT, WHEN MIGHT YOU USE YOUR SKILL?

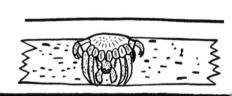

158.

SOME ANIMALS ALIVE TODAY, LIKE WHALES, ARE BIGGER THAN DINOSAURS. WHICH ANIMALS WOULD YOU MOST AND LEAST LIKE TO SEE GROW ENORMOUS?

MOST LIKE TO SEE:

LEAST LIKE TO SEE:

159.

THE WAY THAT THE MOON ROTATES AROUND EARTH MEANS THAT WE ONLY EVER SEE ONE SIDE OF IT. WHAT DO YOU THINK THE OTHER SIDE OF THE MOON LOOKS LIKE? DRAW IT HERE. BE AS SILLY AS YOU LIKE!

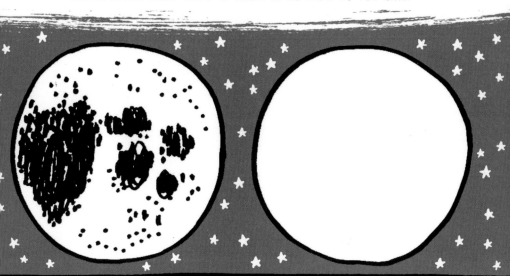

160.

HAVE YOU HEARD OF UNDERWATER KITES? THESE FUNNY-SHAPED KITES ARE TETHERED TO THE OCEAN FLOOR AND USED TO GENERATE ELECTRICITY FROM THE MOVEMENT OF THE TIDES. DRAW SOME FISH AROUND THIS UNDERWATER KITE, AND SOME WAVES ABOVE IT.

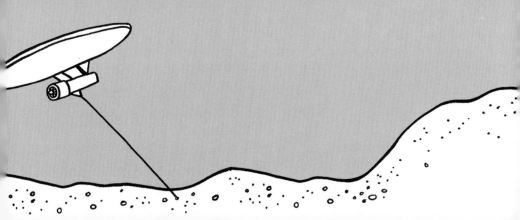

161.

SCIENTISTS CAN SOMETIMES MAKE NEW PLANTS BY "CROSSING" TWO EXISTING PLANTS. MAKE UP A NEW VEGETABLE THAT'S A CROSS BETWEEN TWO REAL VEGETABLES. DRAW YOUR VEGETABLE AND GIVE IT A NAME.

162.

THE BLAST OF AIR FROM A HAIR DRYER CAN KEEP A LIGHT OBJECT, SUCH AS A TISSUE OR A PING-PONG BALL, "FLOATING." DRAW SOMETHING FLOATING IN THE STREAM OF AIR FROM THIS HAIR DRYER.

163.

ALKALI METALS, SUCH AS SODIUM OR POTASSIUM, EXPLODE OR BURN ON CONTACT WITH WATER. YOU WOULDN'T WANT A WATERING CAN MADE FROM THESE METALS! LIST THREE MORE THINGS THAT SHOULDN'T BE MADE FROM AN ALKALI METAL.

1. _____

2. _____

3. _____

164.

IMAGINE YOU HAVE DESIGNED A NEW TYPE OF CAR, WHICH CAN DO SOMETHING AMAZING THAT OTHER CARS CAN'T. WRITE AN AD FOR IT, TELLING PEOPLE WHY THEY SHOULD BUY IT.

165.

JELLYFISH LAKE IN THE PALAU ISLANDS IN THE PACIFIC OCEAN IS HOME TO HUNDREDS OF THOUSANDS OF JELLYFISH. FILL THIS LAKE WITH COLORFUL JELLYFISH.

166.

FOSSILS ARE OFTEN FOUND IN LAYERS OF ROCK CALLED STRATA. THE DEEPER THE FOSSIL, THE OLDER IT IS. COPY THESE FOSSILS ONTO THE LAYERS OF ROCK, MAKING SURE THE OLDEST FOSSIL IS AT THE BOTTOM AND THE YOUNGEST AT THE TOP.

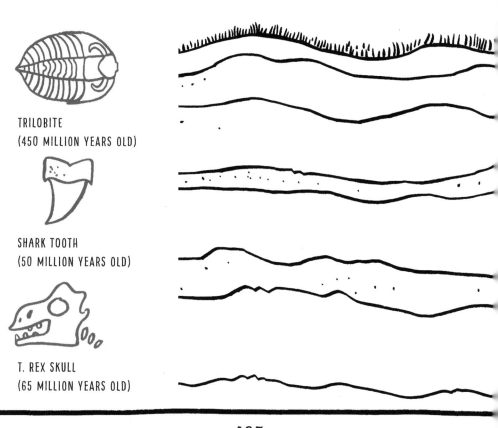

TRILOBITE
(450 MILLION YEARS OLD)

SHARK TOOTH
(50 MILLION YEARS OLD)

T. REX SKULL
(65 MILLION YEARS OLD)

167.

THE FASTEST PLANE EVER MADE WAS POWERED BY A ROCKET AND COULD TRAVEL AT ALMOST 4,500 MPH. IT COULD FLY BETWEEN BOSTON AND MOSCOW IN AN HOUR! WHERE WOULD YOU GO IN A PLANE THAT FAST?

168.

AN IGLOO IS A SHELTER OR HOME MADE FROM BLOCKS OF ICE. EVEN THOUGH ICE IS COLD, IT'S A GOOD INSULATOR, SO IT TRAPS WARMTH INSIDE. DESIGN YOUR OWN ICE HOUSE HERE.

169.

SCOVILLE UNITS MEASURE THE HEAT OF CHILIES. A MILLI-HELEN IS A MEASUREMENT OF BEAUTY. OLFS MEASURE BODY ODOR! IF YOU HAD TO MEASURE HAPPINESS, WHAT UNIT WOULD YOU USE? MAKE IT UP!

170.

THERE IS NO SOUND IN SPACE SINCE THERE IS NO AIR FOR THE SOUND TO TRAVEL THROUGH. WHAT NOISY THING WOULD YOU LIKE TO DO—SILENTLY—ON THE MOON?

171.

SOME BACTERIA REPRODUCE EVERY 20 MINUTES BY SPLITTING IN HALF. FILL THIS SPACE WITH BACTERIA, MAKING EACH GENERATION A DIFFERENT COLOR.

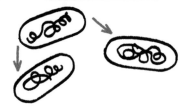

172.

A HOLOGRAM IS A THREE-DIMENSIONAL (3D) IMAGE MADE USING LASERS. IF YOU COULD HAVE A HOLOGRAM PET, WHAT WOULD IT BE?

173.

SOME ANIMALS SEE THE WORLD VERY DIFFERENTLY THAN HUMANS. A DOG'S EYES CAN ONLY DETECT YELLOW, BLUE, AND SHADES OF GRAY. COLOR IN THIS RAINBOW TO SEE WHAT IT MIGHT LOOK LIKE TO A DOG.

KEY:

1. DARK GRAY
2. DARK YELLOW
3. LIGHT YELLOW
4. LIGHT GRAY
5. LIGHT BLUE
6. DARK BLUE
7. DARK GRAY

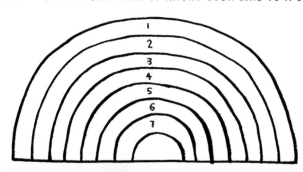

174.

ONE DAY, WE WILL PROBABLY HAVE A RESEARCH STATION ON MARS. IT WILL BE DIFFICULT TO LIVE ON MARS THOUGH, SINCE IT HAS NO BREATHABLE AIR AND GETS VERY COLD. LIST SOME IDEAS FOR HOW WE MIGHT COPE.

175.

SOME ANIMALS HIBERNATE—REST ALL WINTER—AND COME OUT AGAIN IN THE SPRING. IF YOU HIBERNATED ALL WINTER, WHAT WOULD YOU MISS MOST?

176.

THE CORPSE FLOWER IS ONE OF THE WORST-SMELLING PLANTS IN THE WORLD. ITS ROTTING-FLESH SCENT ATTRACTS INSECTS. WHAT WOULD YOU CALL A FLOWER THAT SMELLED LIKE STINKY CHEESE?

177.

ON THE GAS PLANETS JUPITER AND SATURN, IT RAINS DIAMONDS! DRAW YOURSELF HOLDING THIS UMBRELLA IN A DIAMOND RAINSTORM.

178.

FLYING SQUIRRELS HAVE FLAPS THAT HELP THEM GLIDE FROM TREE TO TREE— UNLIKE REGULAR SQUIRRELS WHICH JUST HAVE TO JUMP! WRITE WHAT YOU THINK A FLYING SQUIRREL FEELS WHEN IT'S GLIDING IN THE AIR!

179.

PEOPLE USED TO WRITE USING FEATHERS DIPPED IN INK. NOW WE HAVE ROLLERBALL PENS, IN WHICH THE INK ROLLS OVER A TINY BALL. WHAT NEW TYPE OF PEN MIGHT WE USE IN THE FUTURE? DESCRIBE IT HERE.

180.

HAVE YOU EVER HAD THE HICCUPS? A HICCUP IS A SPASM IN YOUR DIAPHRAGM—
A MUSCLE AT THE BOTTOM OF YOUR CHEST. COMMON "CURES" INCLUDE HOLDING
YOUR BREATH OR GETTING SOMEONE TO MAKE YOU JUMP—BOO! WHAT CURES
WORK FOR YOU? LIST REAL ONES YOU'VE TRIED OR MAKE UP SOME SILLY ONES.

_____

_____

_____

_____

_____

181.

GERMAN-AMERICAN SCIENTIST ALBERT
EINSTEIN ONCE SAID, "THE IMPORTANT
THING IS NOT TO STOP QUESTIONING."
THINK ABOUT A SCIENCE QUESTION
YOU'D LIKE ANSWERED. WRITE IT HERE,
THEN GO AND FIND THE ANSWER!

182.

DO YOU KNOW WHAT A
MILLINILLION IS? IT'S A HUGE
NUMBER—WITH 3,003 ZEROS!
MAKE UP A NAME FOR AN
ENORMOUS NUMBER. HOW
MANY ZEROS DOES IT HAVE?

183.

HEATED LIQUID METAL CAN BE POURED INTO A MOLD. AS IT COOLS, THE METAL HARDENS INTO THE SHAPE OF THE MOLD. DRAW A MOLD FOR A KEY—YOU COULD COPY A REAL ONE OR DESIGN YOUR OWN.

184.

TREES GET MOST OF THE CHEMICALS THEY NEED TO GROW FROM AIR AND WATER. THEY CAN ONLY DO THAT IN SUNLIGHT THOUGH. DRAW A SUN IN THE SKY FOR THIS TREE, AND SOME CLOUDS TO BRING RAIN TO WATER IT.

185.

TANZANITE IS ONE OF THE WORLD'S RAREST GEMSTONES, FOUND ONLY IN TANZANIA. IMAGINE YOU DISCOVER A NEW GEMSTONE THAT IS EVEN RARER, FOUND ONLY IN YOUR BACKYARD! DRAW IT HERE AND GIVE IT A NAME.

186.

AMPHIBIANS ARE BORN WITH GILLS TO BREATHE UNDERWATER. WHEN THEY GROW UP, MANY DEVELOP LUNGS AND BREATHE AIR INSTEAD. IMAGINE IF HUMANS WERE BORN WITH LUNGS BUT GREW GILLS AS ADULTS AND HAD TO MOVE UNDERWATER TO LIVE. WOULD YOU LIKE THIS OR NOT? WRITE YOUR REASONS.

187.

HAVE YOU EVER WISHED ON A STAR? SHOOTING STARS ARE TINY BITS OF ROCK AND DUST THAT MAKE BRIGHT STREAKS IN THE SKY AS THEY BURN UP IN EARTH'S ATMOSPHERE. DRAW A SHOOTING STAR IN THE SKY AND MAKE A WISH ON IT!

188.

A VOLCANOLOGIST IS A SCIENTIST WHO STUDIES VOLCANOES. IMAGINE YOU ARE A VOLCANOLOGIST WHO IS COLLECTING SAMPLES AT A VOLCANO WHEN IT SUDDENLY ERUPTS! WRITE A STORY ABOUT WHAT HAPPENS NEXT.

_____

_____

_____

_____

_____

_____

_____

_____

189.

SCIENTISTS KNOW WHAT DINOSAURS ATE BY STUDYING FOSSILIZED DINOSAUR TEETH, BODIES, AND EVEN POOP! PLANT-EATING DINOSAURS LIKE BRACHYLOPHOSAURUS LOVED TO MUNCH ON FLOWERING PLANTS. DRAW SOME FLOWERS FOR IT TO EAT.

190.

TESSELLATION IS WHEN SHAPES FIT TOGETHER PERFECTLY, WITH NO GAPS. USE A RULER AND A PENCIL TO FINISH OFF THIS TESSELLATING PATTERN, THEN COLOR IT IN.

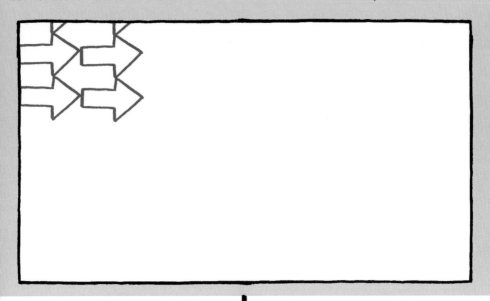

191.

MIRROR WRITING SHOWS A REFLECTION OF NORMAL WRITING—THE LETTERS AND WORDS ARE BACKWARD! WRITE YOUR NAME IN MIRROR WRITING.

192.

THE CHANCE OF YOUR FINGERPRINT BEING IDENTICAL TO SOMEONE ELSE'S IS 1 IN 64 BILLION! DRAW YOUR FINGERPRINT HERE.

193.

THE INTERNATIONAL SPACE STATION IS A LARGE SPACECRAFT THAT
ORBITS EARTH. ASTRONAUTS FROM DIFFERENT COUNTRIES LIVE AND WORK
ON THE STATION. IMAGINE YOU ARE ABOUT TO JOIN THEM FOR THE NEXT SIX
MONTHS! WRITE HOW YOU FEEL AND WHAT YOU ARE EXCITED ABOUT.

194.

GOLD DOESN'T REACT WITH OTHER CHEMICALS, WHICH MEANS IT DOESN'T RUST,
DISSOLVE, OR TARNISH (LOSE ITS SHINE). WHAT WOULD YOU MAKE OUT OF GOLD
SO THAT IT COULD LAST FOREVER?

195.

SOME PLANTS PRODUCE TINY POLLEN GRAINS AS PART OF THEIR WAY OF REPRODUCING. THESE COME IN LOTS OF DIFFERENT SHAPES AND SIZES. DESIGN SOME NEW POLLEN SHAPES AMONG THESE REAL ONES, THEN COLOR THEM ALL IN.

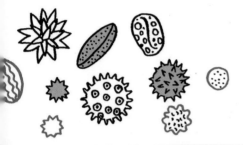

196.

A RAFT FLOATS ON WATER IF IT'S MADE OF MATERIAL LESS DENSE (HEAVY AND COMPACT) THAN WATER. NAME TWO SENSIBLE MATERIALS TO BUILD A RAFT FROM, AND TWO SILLY MATERIALS!

SENSIBLE:

1. _____

2. _____

SILLY:

1. _____

2. _____

197.

YOUR HAIR GROWS ABOUT 6 INCHES A YEAR. IF YOU NEVER CUT IT, AND LIVED UNTIL 90, IT WOULD BE 45 FEET LONG! DRAW YOURSELF WITH REALLY, REALLY LONG HAIR.

198.

AIRPORT SCANNERS USE X-RAYS TO SEE WHAT'S INSIDE A BAG WITHOUT OPENING IT. DRAW SOME ITEMS YOU WOULD TAKE ON VACATION INSIDE THE EMPTY BAG.

199.

IF YOU HAD A ROBOT HELPER, WHAT WOULD YOU LIKE IT TO BE ABLE TO DO?

_____

_____

_____

_____

_____

_____

_____

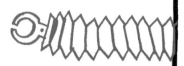

200.

THE AYE-AYE IS AN ANIMAL THAT LIVES IN MADAGASCAR. IT HAS ONE SUPERLONG FINGER THAT IT USES TO FISH OUT BUGS FROM TREE BARK. WHAT WOULD YOU DO WITH A R-E-A-L-L-Y LONG FINGER?

201.

SOME DINOSAURS DEVELOPED SHARP SPIKES, HORNS, AND
TAIL CLUBS TO PROTECT THEMSELVES AGAINST PREDATORS.
GIVE THIS DEFENSELESS DINOSAUR SOME BODY ARMOR!

202.

CRATERS ON THE MOON AND MARS ARE OFTEN NAMED AFTER FAMOUS PEOPLE FROM
HISTORY. WHICH SCIENCE HEROES WOULD YOU NAME THESE FIVE CRATERS AFTER?

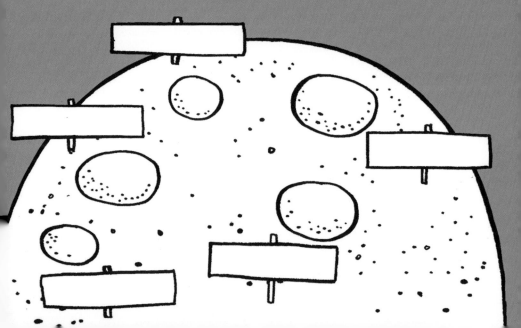

203.

SOME CHEMICALS ARE DANGEROUS. CONTAINERS THAT HOLD THEM HAVE WARNING SYMBOLS LIKE THE ONES SHOWN HERE. MAKE UP YOUR OWN WARNING SYMBOLS FOR THE BOTTLES WITH BLANK LABELS.

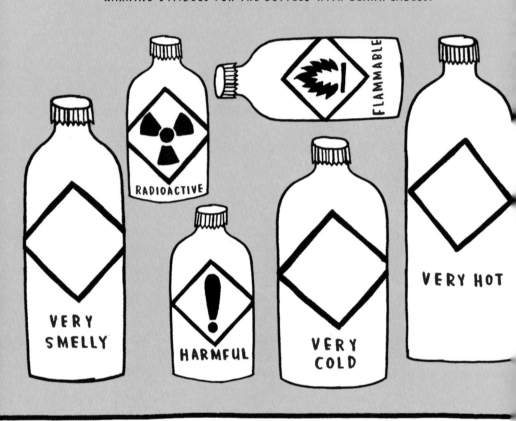

204.

A FEW ANIMALS, INCLUDING CROCODILES AND DOLPHINS, SLEEP WITH ONE EYE OPEN. ONE HALF OF THEIR BRAIN RESTS, WHILE THE OTHER HALF STAYS ALERT! IF HALF OF YOUR BRAIN STAYED AWAKE AT NIGHT, WHAT WOULD YOU DO WITH THE EXTRA TIME?

205.

TEENY FRIDGE MAGNETS ARE MORE POWERFUL THAN GRAVITY! THEY RESIST THE FORCE'S DOWNWARD PULL AND STAY STUCK. DESIGN A FRIDGE MAGNET HERE.

206.

SCIENTISTS STUDYING ELEPHANTS ARE MAKING A DICTIONARY OF "ELEPHANT-SPEAK." WHICH ANIMAL WOULD YOU MOST LIKE TO BE ABLE TO TALK TO?

207.

ROPE IS MADE OF LOTS OF FIBERS TWISTED TOGETHER. THIS MAKES IT STRONGER. THINK OF ONE FUN THING YOU COULD DO, OR A GAME YOU COULD PLAY, WITH THIS LENGTH OF ROPE.

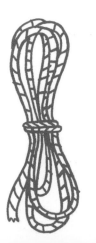

208.

ADRENALINE IS A HORMONE. YOUR BODY PRODUCES ADRENALINE WHEN YOU ARE FRIGHTENED OR EXCITED. IT MAKES YOUR HEART BEAT FASTER! CAN YOU THINK OF A SITUATION THAT WOULD MAKE YOUR BODY PRODUCE ADRENALINE?

209.

WHEN YOU PEDAL A BICYCLE, ENERGY IS TRANSFERRED FROM YOUR MUSCLES TO THE PEDALS, AND FROM THERE TO THE WHEELS. INVENT SOMETHING ELSE THAT COULD BE POWERED BY PEDALS AND DRAW OR DESCRIBE IT HERE.

210.

ALL BIRDS:
- HAVE A BACKBONE
- HAVE FEATHERS
- HAVE WINGS
- LAY EGGS

NAME AS MANY KINDS OF BIRDS AS YOU CAN THINK OF HERE.

211.

ENGLISH MATHEMATICIAN JOHN WALLIS INVENTED THE SYMBOL FOR INFINITY. IT'S USED FOR THINGS THAT GO ON AND ON FOREVER. COME UP WITH A NEW INFINITY SYMBOL AND DRAW IT HERE.

212.

CONSTELLATIONS ARE GROUPS OF STARS THAT FORM A PATTERN IN THE SKY.
CONNECT THE DOTS TO REVEAL A REAL-LIFE CONSTELLATION CALLED DRACO.
WHAT DOES THE PATTERN LOOK LIKE TO YOU—A DRAGON? A FLYING KITE?
SOMETHING ELSE? TURN IT INTO A PICTURE.

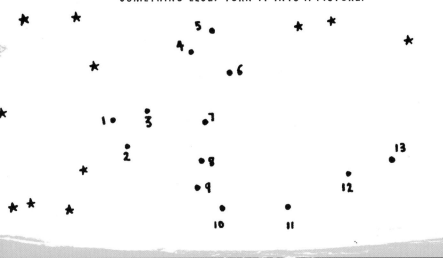

213.

YOU CAN FIND DIFFERENT SHAPES AROUND YOU ALL THE TIME.
LOOK AROUND THE ROOM OR PLACE YOU'RE IN, AND LIST THE
CIRCLES AND RECTANGLES YOU SEE IN THE OBJECTS AROUND YOU.

CIRCLE

RECTANGLE

214.

A WEATHERVANE SHOWS WHICH DIRECTION THE WIND IS BLOWING FROM. THESE DEVICES HAVE BEEN USED SINCE ANCIENT TIMES. MANY HAVE A DECORATION ON TOP, SUCH AS A ROOSTER. DESIGN YOUR OWN WEATHERVANE HERE.

EXAMPLE

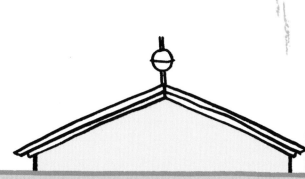

215.

EVERY MINUTE, APPROXIMATELY 250 BABIES ARE BORN AROUND THE WORLD! TIME YOURSELF AND SEE HOW MANY BABIES YOU CAN DRAW IN ONE MINUTE.

216.

OPTICAL ILLUSIONS TRICK OUR BRAINS INTO SEEING THINGS THAT AREN'T ACTUALLY THERE. COLOR IN THIS CANDLESTICK, THEN STEP BACK FROM THE PAGE AND TAKE ANOTHER LOOK—CAN YOU SEE TWO FACES?

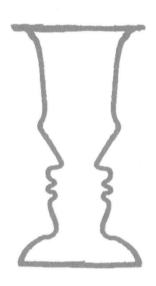

217.

LEFT UNCUT FOR 10 YEARS, YOUR FINGERNAILS WOULD BE OVER 16 INCHES LONG! LIST TWO ADVANTAGES AND TWO DISADVANTAGES OF HAVING SUPERLONG NAILS.

ADVANTAGES:

1. _ _ _ _ _ _ _ _ _ _

_ _ _ _ _ _ _ _ _

2. _ _ _ _ _ _ _ _ _

_ _ _ _ _ _ _ _ _

DISADVANTAGES:

1. _ _ _ _ _ _ _ _ _

_ _ _ _ _ _ _ _ _

2. _ _ _ _ _ _ _ _ _

_ _ _ _ _ _ _ _ _

218.

SCIENTISTS HAVE FOUND THAT SMILING MAKES YOUR BRAIN RELEASE CHEMICALS THAT MAKE YOU FEEL HAPPIER. DRAW A BIG SMILE HERE.

219.

MOST PLANTS NEED SUNLIGHT TO GROW. YOUNG SUNFLOWERS ACTUALLY TURN THEIR HEADS TO FOLLOW THE SUN AS IT TRAVELS ACROSS THE SKY EVERY DAY. FILL THIS FIELD WITH SUNFLOWERS.

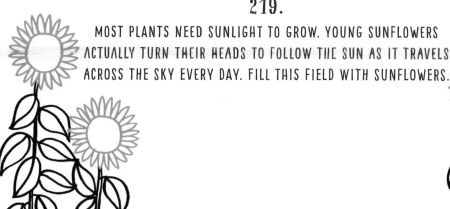

220.

WOOD IS OPAQUE, WHICH MEANS LIGHT CAN'T TRAVEL THROUGH IT. IMAGINE IF IT WAS SEE-THROUGH INSTEAD. WHAT WOULD BE THE BEST THING AND WORST THING ABOUT TAKING A TRIP IN A SEE-THROUGH WOODEN BOAT?

BEST THING: _____

_____

WORST THING: _____

_____

221.

SLEEP IS VERY GOOD FOR YOU; IT GIVES YOUR BODY TIME TO REST, REPAIR, AND REENERGIZE. WHAT HELPS YOU GET A GOOD NIGHT'S SLEEP?

222.

IN THE 1400S, GERMAN INVENTOR JOHANNES GUTENBERG INVENTED THE WORLD'S FIRST MECHANICAL PRINTING PRESS. THIS MEANT BOOKS DIDN'T NEED TO BE COPIED BY HAND, AND MORE BOOKS COULD BE MADE AND SHARED. TODAY, BOOKS ARE EVERYWHERE! WRITE A NOTE TO JOHANNES, THANKING HIM FOR HIS INVENTION.

223.

DNA STANDS FOR DEOXYRIBONUCLEIC ACID. IT'S A CHEMICAL FOUND IN THE CELLS OF ALL LIVING THINGS, INCLUDING YOU. DNA CARRIES THE INFORMATION YOUR BODY NEEDS TO GROW AND FUNCTION. IT LOOKS A BIT LIKE A SPIRAL LADDER. FILL THIS SPACE WITH DRAWINGS OF DNA.

224.

THE WRIGHT BROTHERS ARE FAMOUS FOR INVENTING AND FLYING THE WORLD'S FIRST SUCCESSFUL MOTOR-OPERATED PLANE. THEY DECIDED WHO WOULD MAKE THE FIRST FLIGHT VIA A COIN TOSS! IMAGINE YOU WERE ONE OF THE BROTHERS THAT DAY—WOULD YOU WANT TO WIN THE TOSS? WHY OR WHY NOT?

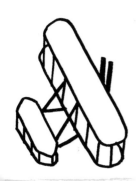

225.

BY USING STRONG MAGNETS THAT REPEL EACH OTHER, THINGS CAN BE MADE TO LEVITATE (HOVER ABOVE THE GROUND). HIGH-SPEED MAGLEV TRAINS WORK THIS WAY, USING MAGNETS ON THE TRACK AND ON THE UNDERSIDE OF THE TRAIN. WHAT WOULD YOU INVENT USING THIS TECHNOLOGY? DRAW IT OR WRITE ABOUT IT.

226.

OFTEN WHEN YOU SEE SOMEONE YAWN, IT MAKES YOU YAWN, TOO—SCIENTISTS AREN'T SURE WHY. WHAT DO YOU THINK COULD BE THE REASON?

227.

AN IRREVERSIBLE REACTION IS SOMETHING THAT CAN'T BE UNDONE, SUCH AS FRYING AN EGG—ONCE FRIED, IT CAN NEVER BE UN-FRIED! DRAW AN UNCOOKED EGG AND A FRIED EGG BELOW.

228.

SOME BEACHES ARE MADE ALMOST ENTIRELY OF FISH POOP! PARROTFISH CRUNCH UP BITS OF CORAL AND POOP IT OUT AS SAND. MAKE UP A NAME FOR A BEACH MADE OF FISH POOP.

229.

THE MILLENNIUM PRIZE PROBLEMS ARE SEVEN MIND-BOGGLING MATH PROBLEMS. SIX REMAIN A MYSTERY. A $1 MILLION PRIZE IS PROMISED TO ANYONE WHO CAN SOLVE ONE. IMAGINE YOU WIN ONE OF THE PRIZES! WHAT HAPPENS NEXT?

230.

DID YOU KNOW THAT ADULT HUMANS HAVE 206 BONES, BUT BABY HUMANS ARE BORN WITH 300 BONES? THIS IS BECAUSE AS CHILDREN GROW, SOME BONES FUSE TOGETHER. INVENT A DIFFERENT REASON FOR WHY THIS HAPPENS.

231.

ON A SPACE STATION, ASTRONAUTS EXPERIENCE WEIGHTLESSNESS, WHICH MAKES EVERYTHING FLOAT AROUND. THINK OF ONE THING THAT WOULD BE HARD TO DO IF YOU, AND EVERYTHING AROUND YOU, WAS FLOATING ABOUT.

232.

A BUTTERFLY CAN TASTE THROUGH SENSORS IN ITS FEET. IF YOU COULD DO THIS TOO, WHICH FOOD WOULD YOU MOST LIKE TO TREAD ON?

233.

IT'S PRETTY IMPOSSIBLE TO DRAW A PERFECT CIRCLE BY HAND— BUT THAT DOESN'T MEAN YOU CAN'T TRY! FILL THIS SPACE WITH CIRCLES, TRYING TO DRAW THEM AS PERFECTLY AS POSSIBLE.

234.

TEST YOUR SHORT-TERM MEMORY! AT THE TOP OF THE PAGE THERE ARE SEVEN OBJECTS. STUDY THEM FOR 1 MINUTE, THEN COVER THEM UP, AND LIST THEM BELOW. CAN YOU REMEMBER THEM ALL?

235.

FIREWORKS GET THEIR COLOR FROM CHEMICALS THAT ARE MIXED WITH EXPLOSIVES. MAKE UP A FIREWORK NAME BY CHOOSING A WORD FROM EACH COLUMN IN THE TABLE BELOW, THEN DRAW YOUR EXPLODING FIREWORK.

CRACKLE	VOLCANO
HOWLING	DRAGON
MIGHTY	COMET
DANCING	BOOM
FIERY	WHIRLWIND

MY FIREWORK NAME IS: _____ _____

236.

A GOOGOL IS A VERY BIG NUMBER:
A 1 FOLLOWED BY 100 ZEROS.
WRITE A GOOGOL IN THIS SPACE.

237.

WHEN SCOTTISH INVENTOR ALEXANDER GRAHAM BELL MADE THE FIRST EVER PHONE CALL, HE SAID, "MR. WATSON, COME HERE—I WANT TO SEE YOU." (HIS ASSISTANT, MR. WATSON, WAS ON THE OTHER END OF THE CALL.) WHAT WOULD YOU HAVE SAID?

238.

SOME SAND IS MADE OF SHELLS FROM TINY CREATURES CALLED FORAMINIFERA. THE MICROSCOPIC SHELLS COME IN MANY DIFFERENT SHAPES. MAKE UP SOME SHELL DESIGNS OF YOUR OWN AND DRAW THEM HERE.

239.

ONE TYPE OF JELLYFISH CAN CHANGE FROM AN ADULT BACK INTO ITS BABY STATE, CALLED A POLYP, AND START LIFE AGAIN. WOULD YOU LIKE TO BE ABLE TO DO THIS OR NOT? WRITE YOUR REASONS WHY.

240.

YOUR BODY IS FULL OF GOOD BACTERIA, WHICH HELP DIGEST FOOD AND TAKE IN NUTRIENTS, AND BAD BACTERIA, WHICH CAN CAUSE ILLNESS AND DISEASE. DRAW WHAT YOU THINK GOOD BACTERIA AND BAD BACTERIA LOOK LIKE.

241.

THE LOWER GRAVITY ON THE MOON MEANS YOU CAN THROW THINGS FARTHER, JUMP HIGHER, AND LEAP LONGER DISTANCES. WHICH TRACK-AND-FIELD ATHLETICS EVENT WOULD YOU MOST LIKE TO TRY OUT ON THE MOON?

242.

ROLLER COASTERS DON'T HAVE ENGINES. A MOTOR PULLS THE CARS UP THE FIRST SLOPE. AS THE CARS GO UP, THEY GAIN POTENTIAL ENERGY, THEN GRAVITY PULLS THEM DOWN! WHEN THEY GO DOWN, THEY GAIN KINETIC ENERGY WHICH PUSHES THEM UP THE NEXT SLOPE, AND ON AND ON IT GOES! DRAW SOME CARS AND PEOPLE ON THIS ROLLER COASTER.

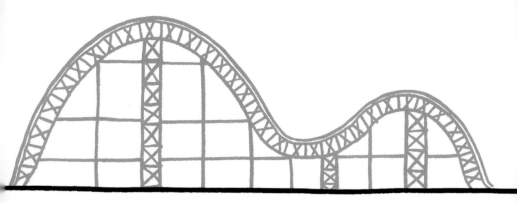

243.

THERE ARE 118 CHEMICAL ELEMENTS. THESE ARE BASIC CHEMICAL INGREDIENTS THAT EVERYTHING IN THE UNIVERSE IS MADE FROM. SOME ARE SOLIDS (LIKE IRON), SOME ARE GASES (LIKE OXYGEN), AND A COUPLE ARE LIQUIDS (LIKE MERCURY). IMAGINE YOU HAVE DISCOVERED A NEW CHEMICAL ELEMENT. DESCRIBE IT HERE.

NAME:_____

SOLID, LIQUID, OR GAS? _____

COLOR: _____

SPECIAL PROPERTIES OR USES: _____

_____

244.

RECYCLING IS WHEN A WASTE MATERIAL THAT YOU NO LONGER NEED OR USE IS TURNED INTO SOMETHING NEW. PLASTIC IS OFTEN RECYCLED INTO ALL KINDS OF THINGS. DESIGN SOMETHING RECYCLED FROM PLASTIC BAGS HERE.

245.

ASTRONAUTS HEADING TO SPACE TAKE A PERSONAL PREFERENCE KIT, A SMALL CONTAINER THAT HOLDS ALL THEIR PERSONAL ITEMS. IF YOU COULD ONLY TAKE THREE POSSESSIONS TO SPACE, WHAT WOULD THEY BE?

1. _____

2. _____

3. _____

246.

LIGHTNING HEATS THE AIR IT PASSES THROUGH TO 50,000 DEGREES FAHRENHEIT—THAT'S FIVE TIMES HOTTER THAN THE SURFACE OF THE SUN! DRAW SOME LIGHTNING FORKING DOWN TO THE GROUND. WHERE WILL IT HIT?

247.

A PENTAGON IS A SHAPE WITH FIVE SIDES. MAKE A DRAWING USING THIS PENTAGON.

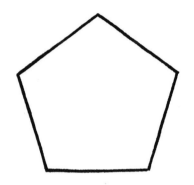

248.

ENGINEERS ARE WORKING ON MAKING SELF-DRIVING CARS. WHAT DO YOU THINK WOULD BE GOOD ABOUT THIS INVENTION AND WHAT WOULD BE BAD?

GOOD:

BAD:

249.

OUR PLANET IS MADE OF SEVERAL LAYERS. COLOR IN THIS PICTURE OF EARTH, MAKING EACH LAYER A DIFFERENT COLOR OR PATTERN.

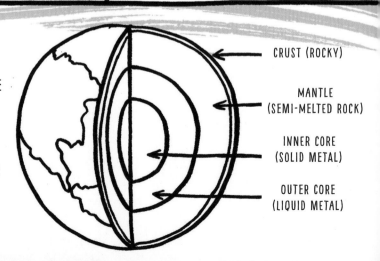

CRUST (ROCKY)

MANTLE (SEMI-MELTED ROCK)

INNER CORE (SOLID METAL)

OUTER CORE (LIQUID METAL)

250.

TODAY, MOST DYES ARE SYNTHETIC (MAN-MADE IN LABS), BUT IN THE PAST, DYES WERE MADE FROM CHEMICALS FOUND IN NATURE. THESE PLANTS, FRUITS, AND VEGETABLES CAN ALL BE USED AS NATURAL DYES—COLOR THEM IN!

251.

MOST COMPUTER KEYBOARDS USE THE SAME ARRANGEMENT OF KEYS AS WERE USED ON TYPEWRITERS OVER 100 YEARS AGO. DESIGN A NEW LAYOUT FOR THE LETTERS. THEY COULD GO IN ALPHABETICAL ORDER, OR WITH YOUR FAVORITE LETTERS AT THE TOP!

MOST COMMON ARRANGEMENT

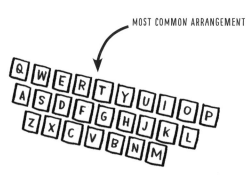

252.

DO YOU KNOW HOW HOT-AIR BALLOONS WORK? HOT AIR RISES, SO WHEN A BURNER HEATS THE AIR INSIDE THE BALLOON, THE HOT AIR CAUSES THE BALLOON TO RISE UP, TOO. COLOR THE HOT-AIR BALLOON HOWEVER YOU LIKE.

253.

SOME ANIMALS GO THROUGH A METAMORPHOSIS, WHERE THEIR BODIES AND FEATURES TRANSFORM. TADPOLES, FOR EXAMPLE, TRANSFORM INTO FROGS. IMAGINE YOU TRANSFORM ONE DAY, AND WAKE UP WITH A DIFFERENT BODY, OR A NEW FEATURE. DESCRIBE YOUR NEW SELF!

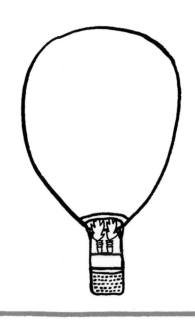

254.

SOME ROCKS HAVE SPECIAL PROPERTIES, SUCH AS BEING MAGNETIC OR ABLE TO FLOAT ON WATER. IMAGINE YOU PICK UP A PEBBLE AND IT CAN DO SOMETHING SUPERSPECIAL! WHAT CAN IT DO?

255.

SOME STONE, SUCH AS FLINT, FLAKES EASILY, AND PEOPLE HAVE USED IT TO MAKE TOOLS LIKE ARROWHEADS AND KNIVES. WHAT TYPE OF TOOL WOULD YOU LIKE TO MAKE FROM THIS STONE? DESCRIBE OR DRAW IT HERE.

256.

SCIENTISTS IN SINGAPORE ARE WORKING ON "CYBORG" COCKROACHES. EACH REAL-LIFE COCKROACH IS FITTED WITH A TINY CAMERA "BACKPACK." IT'S HOPED THE BUGS COULD BE USED TO SEARCH DANGEROUS PLACES, SUCH AS DISASTER SITES. DRAW A CAMERA BACKPACK ON THIS COCKROACH.

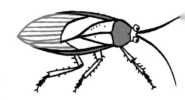

257.

FOOTPRINTS LEFT ON THE MOON BY ASTRONAUTS WILL NEVER DISAPPEAR BECAUSE THERE'S NO WIND OR RAIN TO WASH THEM AWAY. IF YOU COULD WRITE A MESSAGE ON THE MOON THAT WOULD NEVER FADE AWAY, WHAT WOULD IT SAY?

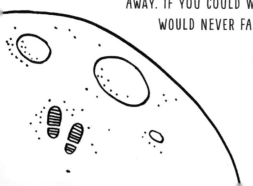

258.

COGS ARE WHEELS WITH "TEETH" THAT ALLOW THEM TO SLOT TOGETHER. WHEN ONE COG IS TURNED, IT TURNS THE OTHERS. COGS ARE FOUND IN ALL KINDS OF MACHINES. ADD MORE COGS TO THE ONES BELOW. IF YOU LIKE, YOU COULD ADD ARROWS TO SHOW THE DIRECTION EACH COG MOVES IN, TOO.

259.

THE AIRWAYS IN YOUR LUNGS HAVE A BRANCHING SHAPE. THEY SPLIT OFF INTO SMALLER AND SMALLER TUBES, JUST LIKE TREE BRANCHES. DRAW THE MISSING AIRWAYS IN THIS LUNG.

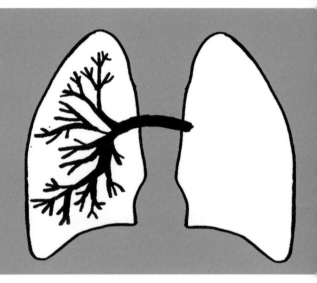

260.

WATER GOES AROUND AND AROUND IN A CYCLE. IT FALLS AS RAIN, PASSES THROUGH PLANTS AND ANIMALS, FLOWS INTO RIVERS AND THE OCEAN, EVAPORATES TO FORM CLOUDS ... THEN GOES AROUND AGAIN! DRINK A GLASS OF WATER. WRITE WHERE YOU THINK THE WATER MIGHT HAVE TRAVELED BEFORE ARRIVING IN YOUR FAUCET.

261.

ABOUT ¾ OF YOUR BRAIN IS MADE UP OF WATER! COLOR IN THE BRAIN BELOW SO IT'S ¾ BLUE AND ¼ RED.

262.

EARTH IS THE ONLY PLANET IN OUR SOLAR SYSTEM NOT NAMED AFTER A GREEK OR ROMAN GOD. "EARTH" SIMPLY MEANS "THE GROUND." RENAME OUR PLANET SOMETHING A LITTLE MORE EXCITING.

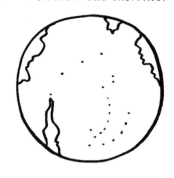

- - - - - - - - - -

263.

ANIMALS USE THEIR TAILS TO HOLD THINGS, OR TO CLIMB, OR LIKE A SCARF TO KEEP THEM WARM AS THEY SLEEP. IF YOU HAD A TAIL, WHAT WOULD YOU USE IT FOR? DRAW IT HERE.

264.

IN THE SUMMER, THE NORTH POLE GETS 24 HOURS OF LIGHT, WHILE IN THE WINTER, IT GETS 24 HOURS OF DARKNESS. WRITE A POSTCARD ABOUT IT BEING ALWAYS LIGHT—OR ALWAYS DARK.

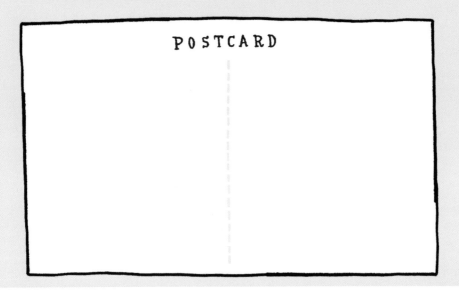

POSTCARD

265.

ENGLISH SCIENTIST ISAAC NEWTON'S "THIRD LAW OF MOTION" SAYS THAT EVERY ACTION MUST HAVE AN EQUAL AND OPPOSITE REACTION. FOR EXAMPLE, WHEN YOU BLOW UP A BALLOON AND THEN LET GO OF IT, THE AIR RUSHES OUT (ACTION) AND THE BALLOON ZOOMS OFF IN THE OPPOSITE DIRECTION (REACTION). FILL THIS SPACE WITH MORE BALLOONS ZIPPING AND ZOOMING, AND THE AIR LEAVING THEM.

266.

AIR IS AN EXCELLENT INSULATOR—IT'S GOOD AT KEEPING HEAT IN.
INSULATED GLASS WINDOWS TRAP A LAYER OF AIR BETWEEN TWO PANES
OF GLASS. A DOWN COMFORTER COMBINES FEATHERS AND AIR FOR WARMTH.
INVENT A PIECE OF CLOTHING THAT USES AIR TO KEEP YOU WARM.

267.

ROCKS CAN BE WEATHERED (WORN AWAY) BY WIND AND RAIN. SOMETIMES, ONE
PART OF THE ROCK IS MORE EASILY WORN AWAY THAN OTHER PARTS. THIS CREATES
AMAZING SHAPES. DRAW SOME MORE UNUSUAL ROCK SHAPES HERE.

268.

SOMEONE WHO IS NEARSIGHTED HAS TROUBLE FOCUSING ON DISTANT OBJECTS. SOMEONE WHO IS FARSIGHTED HAS TROUBLE FOCUSING ON OBJECTS CLOSE-UP. FORTUNATELY, GLASSES CAN CORRECT BOTH PROBLEMS! DRAW SOME GLASSES ON THIS FACE.

269.

RAIN FALLS WHEN TINY DROPLETS OF WATER IN CLOUDS CLUMP TOGETHER AND BECOME TOO HEAVY TO STAY UP IN THE AIR. DRAW SOME MORE PLUMP RAINDROPS FALLING—GIVE THEM FACES, TOO!

270.

IF SOMETHING IS SOLAR POWERED, IT MEANS IT MOVES OR WORKS USING ENERGY FROM THE SUN. THERE ARE SOLAR-POWERED PLANES, LAMPS, WATCHES, AND EVEN SOLAR-POWERED TENTS THAT YOU CAN USE TO CHARGE DEVICES LIKE CELL PHONES OR CAMERAS! WHAT OBJECT DO YOU WISH WAS SOLAR POWERED? WHY?

271.

ANIMALS HAVE OFTEN BEEN USED IN MEDICINE. MAGGOTS CAN EAT THE ROTTING FLESH AROUND A WOUND, AND SNAIL SLIME IS AN OLD TREATMENT FOR BURNS. WHICH OF THESE TREATMENTS WOULD YOU RATHER TRY, AND WHY?

272.

THINK OF AN IMAGINATIVE USE FOR CUSTARD. REMEMBER, IT IS A "THIXOTROPIC" FLUID, WHICH MEANS IT IS VISCOUS (THICK) NORMALLY, BUT BECOMES THINNER WHEN IT IS DISTURBED OR STIRRED.

273.

EPHEMERAL LAKES ARE PRESENT FOR ONLY SHORT PERIODS, AFTER HEAVY RAINFALL, AND ARE MOSTLY DRY THE REST OF THE TIME. IMAGINE YOU DISCOVER A LAKE THAT FORMS ONCE A YEAR. WRITE ABOUT IT HERE. WHERE IS IT? WHEN DOES IT FORM? FOR HOW LONG?

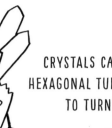

274.

CRYSTALS CAN BE LOTS OF SHAPES, INCLUDING CUBES AND HEXAGONAL TUBES. COLOR IN THE CRYSTALS, THEN ADD DETAILS TO TURN THEM INTO LITTLE CRYSTAL CHARACTERS.

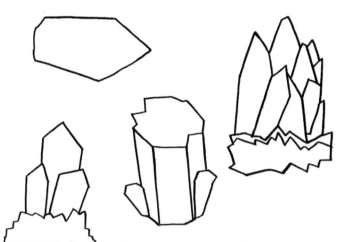

275.

GREEN IS THE RAREST EYE COLOR IN THE WORLD. WHAT COLOR ARE YOUR EYES? COLOR IN THE EYE BELOW TO MATCH YOUR OWN.

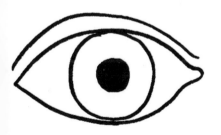

276.

POLISH-FRENCH SCIENTIST MARIE CURIE DISCOVERED THE CHEMICAL ELEMENTS RADIUM AND POLONIUM. SHE NAMED POLONIUM AFTER HER HOME COUNTRY, POLAND. MAKE UP A NAME FOR A NEW ELEMENT, BASED ON THE TOWN WHERE YOU LIVE.

277.

CHALLENGER DEEP IS THE DEEPEST PART OF EARTH'S OCEANS. IT'S AROUND 35,800 FEET (ALMOST 7 MILES!) BENEATH THE SURFACE OF THE PACIFIC OCEAN. A FEW PEOPLE HAVE VISITED IN TINY, CRAMPED SUBMARINES CALLED SUBMERSIBLES. IMAGINE YOU ARE VISITING CHALLENGER DEEP. WRITE ABOUT HOW YOU FEEL AS YOU DESCEND INTO THE DARKNESS.

278.

"EUREKA!" IS WHAT ANCIENT SCIENTIST ARCHIMEDES IS SAID TO HAVE SHOUTED WHEN HE FIGURED OUT THE ANSWER TO A SCIENCE PROBLEM. THE GREEK WORD MEANS "I HAVE FOUND." WHAT WORD WOULD YOU SHOUT IF YOU SOLVED A GREAT SCIENCE MYSTERY?

EUREKA!

279.

SOME BUGS GLOW IN THE DARK, MAKING THEIR OWN LIGHT IN A CHEMICAL PROCESS CALLED BIOLUMINESCENCE. DESIGN YOUR OWN GLOWING BUG.

280.

FOOD SCIENTISTS MAKE SURE FOODS ARE SAFE AND HEALTHY. THEY ALSO DEVELOP NEW FOODS. INVENT A NEW FOOD PRODUCT.

NAME: _ _ _ _ _ _ _ _

FLAVOR: _ _ _ _ _ _ _

MAIN INGREDIENT: _ _ _ _ _ _

_ _ _ _ _ _ _ _

_ _ _ _ _ _ _ _

281.

VENUS HAS A PERMANENT, THICK LAYER OF CLOUD. IF YOU LIVED ON A PLANET LIKE VENUS, WHAT WOULD YOU MISS MOST ABOUT NOT BEING ABLE TO SEE THE SUN OR NIGHT SKY?

282.

THINK ABOUT PLANTS AND ANIMALS IN NATURE. HOW DO THEY PROTECT THEMSELVES FROM PREDATORS OR THE ELEMENTS? GIVE THIS HUMAN HAND A SPECIAL FEATURE INSPIRED BY NATURAL DEFENSES. MAYBE IT HAS SPIKY SPINES LIKE A CACTUS, OR CLAWS LIKE A BEAR?

283.

NASA HAS SENT FIVE ROBOTIC VEHICLES, CALLED ROVERS, TO MARS. THEY WERE NAMED SOJOURNER, SPIRIT, OPPORTUNITY, CURIOSITY, AND PERSEVERANCE. WHAT WOULD YOU NAME THE NEXT ROVER?

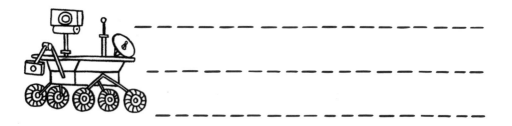

_ _ _ _ _ _ _ _ _ _ _ _ _ _ _ _

_ _ _ _ _ _ _ _ _ _ _ _ _ _ _ _

_ _ _ _ _ _ _ _ _ _ _ _ _

284.

MILLIPEDES GROW MORE LEGS AS THEY GET BIGGER. EACH TIME THEY SHED THEIR SKIN, THEY ADD FURTHER BODY SEGMENTS, WITH MORE LEGS. WHAT WOULD YOU LOOK LIKE IF YOU ADDED EXTRA LEGS AS YOU GREW? DRAW YOURSELF WITH FOUR EXTRA LEGS!

285.

THE ELECTRIC LIGHTBULB WAS INVENTED IN THE 19TH CENTURY. AMERICAN THOMAS EDISON MADE THE FIRST PRACTICAL LIGHTBULB THAT COULD BE USED IN THE HOME. IMAGINE A WORLD WITHOUT ELECTRIC LIGHT! WHAT WOULD YOU NO LONGER BE ABLE TO DO? LIST THE THINGS YOU'D REALLY MISS.

286.

HURRICANES ARE TROPICAL STORMS WITH DESTRUCTIVE HIGH WINDS. EACH HURRICANE IS GIVEN A NAME SO THAT SCIENTISTS CAN STUDY AND KEEP TRACK OF THEM. THE FIRST HURRICANE OF THE YEAR STARTS WITH THE LETTER A (SUCH AS ANDREA), THE NEXT STARTS WITH THE LETTER B (SUCH AS BRAD), AND SO ON, IN ALPHABETICAL ORDER. THE NAMES ALTERNATE BETWEEN FEMALE AND MALE. PICK NAMES FOR THE FIRST 10 HURRICANES OF NEXT YEAR.

A: _ _ _ _ _ _ _ _   F: _ _ _ _ _ _ _ _

B: _ _ _ _ _ _ _   G: _ _ _ _ _ _ _ _

C: _ _ _ _ _ _ _ _   H: _ _ _ _ _ _ _ _

D: _ _ _ _ _ _ _ _   I: _ _ _ _ _ _ _ _

E: _ _ _ _ _ _ _   J: _ _ _ _ _ _ _ _

287.

FERTILIZERS ARE ADDED TO SOIL TO MAKE PLANTS GROW WELL. IN THE PAST, BIRD DROPPINGS CALLED "GUANO" WERE USED FOR FERTILIZER. IMAGINE IT WAS YOUR JOB TO DIG OUT MOUNTAINS OF BIRD DROPPINGS. WRITE ABOUT YOUR STINKY JOB.

288.

YOUR SHADOW ALWAYS FALLS ON THE SIDE OF YOU THAT'S AWAY FROM THE SUN SINCE IT'S MADE BY YOUR BODY BLOCKING THE PATH OF THE SUNLIGHT. DRAW THIS DOG'S SHADOW IN THE RIGHT PLACE.

289.

FAMOUS ENGLISH FOSSIL HUNTER MARY ANNING FOUND THE SKULL OF AN ANCIENT REPTILE CALLED AN ICHTHYOSAUR WHEN SHE WAS JUST 12 YEARS OLD. IMAGINE YOU ARE HER—WRITE A LETTER TO A FRIEND DESCRIBING WHAT HAPPENED AND HOW YOU FELT.

290.

DID YOU KNOW THAT SNOW CAN BE PINK? "WATERMELON SNOW" IS CAUSED BY MICROSCOPIC PINK ALGAE THAT GROW AS THE SNOW STARTS TO MELT. DRAW A PINK SNOWMAN BELOW!

291.

INVENTORS OFTEN START WITH A PROBLEM THEY WANT TO SOLVE AND THEN INVENT SOMETHING TO FIX IT. LIST THREE PROBLEMS YOU'D LIKE TO SEE FIXED.

1. _ _ _ _ _ _ _ _ _

_ _ _ _ _ _ _ _ _

2. _ _ _ _ _ _ _ _ _

_ _ _ _ _ _ _ _ _

3. _ _ _ _ _ _ _ _ _

_ _ _ _ _ _ _ _ _

292.

A SPIRAL IS A LINE THAT GOES AROUND A POINT IN A CIRCLE, GETTING FARTHER AND FARTHER AWAY FROM THE MIDDLE. FILL THIS SPACE WITH MORE SPIRALS.

293.

PLANETS FORM AS SMALL LUMPS OF ROCK AND ICE CRASH INTO EACH OTHER AND JOIN TOGETHER. DRAW THE STAGES OF A PLANET FORMING.

STAGE 1 (SEPARATE LUMPS OF ROCK AND ICE)

STAGE 2 (LUMPS COLLIDE)

STAGE 3 (NEW PLANET FORMED)

294.

NOBEL PRIZES ARE IMPORTANT AWARDS THAT ARE GIVEN OUT EVERY YEAR. THREE OF THE PRIZES ARE FOR PHYSICS, CHEMISTRY, AND MEDICINE. WHICH WOULD YOU MOST LIKE TO WIN?

ALFRED NOBEL

295.

AS TECHNOLOGY DEVELOPS, SO DO WE! BEFORE PLANES, THERE WERE NO PILOTS, AND BEFORE CAMERAS THERE WERE NO PHOTOGRAPHERS. MAKE UP A JOB THAT MIGHT EXIST 100 YEARS FROM NOW.

296.

A PULLEY IS A SIMPLE MACHINE WHICH CAN LIFT HEAVY LOADS USING A ROPE LOOPED OVER A WHEEL. DRAW SOMETHING HEAVIER THAN A DOG IN THE EMPTY BASKET THAT'S RAISING THE DOG OFF THE GROUND.

297.

UNDER THE SOIL IS THE "WATER TABLE," WHERE SPACES BETWEEN ROCK ARE FILLED WITH WATER. IF YOU DIG A DEEP ENOUGH HOLE, EVENTUALLY YOU'LL FIND WATER AT THE BOTTOM. WRITE A STORY ABOUT DIGGING A HOLE AND FINDING SOMETHING STRANGE FLOATING IN THE WATER AT THE BOTTOM OF IT.

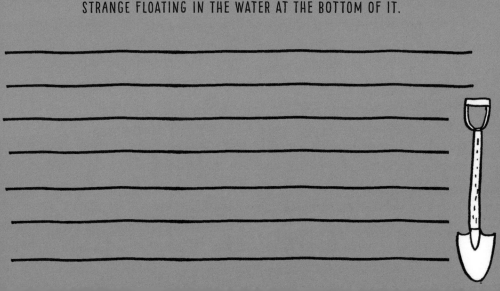

298.

GEOMETRY IS THE STUDY OF SHAPES, LINES, AND ANGLES. IRANIAN MATHEMATICIAN MARYAM MIRZAKHANI IS THE ONLY WOMAN TO WIN THE FIELDS MEDAL, THE MOST IMPORTANT PRIZE IN MATH, FOR HER WORK ON CURVY SHAPES. DRAW A CURVY SHAPE HERE AND GIVE IT A NAME!

299.

STALACTITES FORM ON THE CEILINGS OF CAVES AS WATER CONTAINING MINERALS DRIPS FROM ABOVE. THEY GROW VERY SLOWLY—ABOUT HALF AN INCH EVERY 100 YEARS. TURN THIS STALACTITE INTO THE FACE OF AN OLD MAN WITH A LONG BEARD!

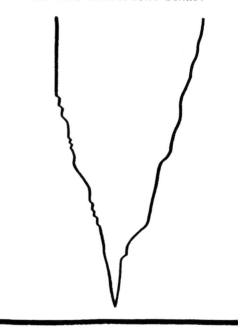

300.

ON EARTH, THE SKY IS BLUE IN THE DAY AND REDDISH-ORANGE AT SUNSET. ON MARS, THE SKY IS THE COLOR OF BUTTERSCOTCH (YELLOWISH-BROWN) IN THE DAY AND GLOWS BLUE AT SUNSET! COLOR THIS SKY ON MARS.

301.

IN 1996 A MACHINE CALLED DEEP BLUE DEFEATED GARRY KASPAROV—THE WORLD CHESS CHAMPION AT THE TIME—IN A GAME OF CHESS. WRITE A NEWSPAPER HEADLINE ANNOUNCING THE NEWS... USING ONLY THREE WORDS!

302.

A FOOD CHAIN SHOWS WHAT EATS WHAT IN THE NATURAL WORLD—FOR EXAMPLE, A LEAF CAN BE EATEN BY A CATERPILLAR, WHICH CAN BE EATEN BY A BIRD. COMPLETE THE THREE FOOD CHAINS BELOW, HOWEVER YOU LIKE!

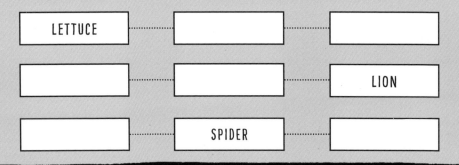

LETTUCE		
		LION
	SPIDER	

303.

ELECTRONIC DEVICES CONTAIN ELECTRICAL CIRCUITS PRINTED ONTO PIECES OF PLASTIC. THESE CIRCUITS ARE ROUTES FOR ELECTRICITY TO MOVE AROUND, AND THEY LOOK A BIT LIKE MAPS. ADD TO THIS CIRCUIT TO FILL THE SPACE.

304.

A HELICOPTER FLIES USING SPINNING BLADES CALLED ROTORS, WHICH LIFT IT OFF THE GROUND. IT CAN GO STRAIGHT UP AND DOWN, SO IT CAN LAND IN SMALL SPACES. WHERE WOULD YOU LIKE TO GO IN A HELICOPTER?

305.

SCIENTISTS CAN LEARN A LOT ABOUT LONG-DEAD ANIMALS FROM THEIR FOSSILIZED POOP, INCLUDING WHAT THEY ATE. WHAT MIGHT A SCIENTIST FROM THE FUTURE LEARN ABOUT YOU FROM YOUR FOSSILIZED POOP? LIST EVERYTHING YOU'VE EATEN IN THE LAST 24 HOURS.

_____

_____

_____

_____

_____

_____

_____

306.

THE CELLS IN OUR BODIES COME IN LOTS OF DIFFERENT SHAPES. MAKE UP SOME NEW SHAPES FOR DIFFERENT CELLS.

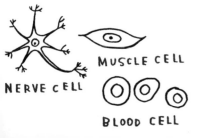

NERVE CELL

MUSCLE CELL

BLOOD CELL

307.

A SHEEP CALLED DOLLY, BORN IN 1996, WAS THE FIRST CLONE OF AN ADULT MAMMAL. A CLONE IS AN EXACT COPY OF A LIVING THING. CAN YOU DRAW AN IDENTICAL SHEEP NEXT TO DOLLY?

308.

ARCHEOLOGISTS ARE SCIENTISTS WHO STUDY HUMAN HISTORY BY FINDING AND ANALYZING ANCIENT SITES AND ARTIFACTS SUCH AS TOOLS, WEAPONS, CLOTHES, JEWELS—EVEN TOYS! IMAGINE YOU DIG UP AN ANCIENT TOY IN YOUR BACKYARD. DRAW IT AND DESCRIBE HOW OLD IT IS AND WHO MIGHT HAVE USED IT.

309.

SOME FLEAS CAN JUMP ABOUT 100 TIMES THEIR BODY LENGTH. THAT'S LIKE YOU JUMPING OVER A 30-STORY BUILDING! DRAW SOMETHING VERY TALL FOR THIS CHILD TO JUMP OVER.

310.

GEORGE WASHINGTON CARVER WAS AN AMERICAN SCIENTIST AND INVENTOR. HE INVENTED HUNDREDS OF FOOD PRODUCTS ALL MADE USING PEANUTS, FROM PEANUT MILK TO PEANUT OIL! CAN YOU INVENT 3 FOODS MADE FROM GRAPES?

311.

WHAT WORDS DO YOU THINK OF WHEN YOU READ THE WORD "SCIENCE"? LIST THEM HERE.

312.

ICE SKATES GLIDE EASILY OVER THE ICE BECAUSE THE TOP LAYER OF THE ICE BEHAVES LIKE WATER, SO IT'S SUPER SLIPPERY. DRAW THE PATTERN YOU WOULD TRACE ON THIS ICE IF YOU WERE AN ICE SKATER.

313.

CHILDREN NORMALLY HAVE 20 BABY TEETH, WHICH ARE REPLACED BY 32 ADULT TEETH. HOW MANY TEETH DO YOU HAVE? WRITE THE NUMBER HERE.

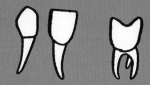

314.

THE ONLY THING THAT CAN SCRATCH A DIAMOND IS ANOTHER DIAMOND— IT'S THE HARDEST MATERIAL IN THE WORLD. TURN THIS SPARKLING DIAMOND INTO A PIECE OF JEWELRY.

315.

OUR SENSE OF BALANCE IS CALLED "EQUILIBRIOCEPTION." WITHOUT IT, WE WOULD FALL OVER ALL THE TIME! HOW LONG CAN YOU STAND ON ONE LEG WITH YOUR EYES CLOSED? RECORD YOUR TIME HERE.

316.

TEST TUBES ARE GLASS CONTAINERS, USED DURING SCIENCE EXPERIMENTS. FILL THIS TEST TUBE AND LABEL WHAT'S INSIDE.

317.

FROM HOVERBOARDS TO HANG GLIDERS, LOTS OF MACHINES HAVE BEEN INVENTED THAT CAN FLY. GIVE YOURSELF ONE MINUTE TO WRITE AS MANY AS YOU CAN THINK OF.

318.

SOME PEOPLE THINK THAT IF WE COULD TRAVEL FAST ENOUGH, WE COULD GO BACKWARD THROUGH TIME. WHAT TIME IN THE PAST WOULD YOU LIKE TO VISIT IF YOU HAD A TIME MACHINE?

319.

IF YOU DROP A ROCK INTO SOME WATER, THE ROCK PUSHES THE WATER OUT OF THE WAY, CREATING RIPPLES AND A SPLASH. THE BIGGER THE ROCK, THE BIGGER THE SPLASH! DRAW A ROCK DROPPING INTO A PUDDLE.

320.

SPORTS SCIENTISTS USE THEIR KNOWLEDGE OF HOW THE HUMAN BODY WORKS TO IMPROVE THE PERFORMANCE OF ATHLETES. IF YOU WERE A SPORTS SCIENTIST, WHICH SPORT WOULD YOU MOST LIKE TO WORK IN? WHY?

321.

SOME NIGHT VISION GOGGLES LET YOU SEE IN THE DARK, BY INTENSIFYING THE VERY FAINT LIGHT THERE IS. THEY SHOW AN IMAGE IN GREEN AND BLACK. USE GREEN AND BLACK TO DRAW WHAT YOU MIGHT SEE IF YOU WENT OUTSIDE YOUR HOME IN THE DARK.

322.

A METAL DETECTOR WORKS BY BEAMING WAVES OF ENERGY INTO THE GROUND. IF THESE HIT A METAL OBJECT, A SLIGHTLY DIFFERENT WAVE OF ENERGY COMES BACK, WHICH THE DETECTOR PICKS UP. METAL DETECTORS HAVE UNEARTHED COINS, JEWELRY, AND EVEN CROWNS—AS WELL AS OLD METAL TRASH. DRAW SOME THINGS FOR THIS METAL DETECTOR TO FIND.

323.

A MONKEY'S FEET ARE STRONG AND FLEXIBLE ENOUGH TO GRIP BRANCHES AND HOLD FOOD. HOW STRONG AND FLEXIBLE ARE YOUR FEET? PICK SOMETHING UP WITH YOUR TOES AND RECORD HOW LONG YOU CAN HOLD IT FOR!

324.

DRAW A T-SHIRT DESIGN INSPIRED BY SCIENCE.

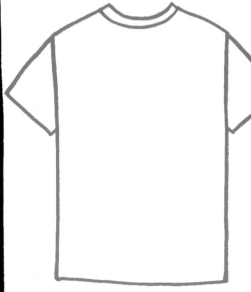

325.

FRENCH CHEMIST LOUIS PASTEUR DISCOVERED THAT HEATING UP LIQUID KILLS THE GERMS IN IT. THIS PROCESS IS CALLED PASTEURIZATION (NAMED AFTER PASTEUR), AND IS USED TO MAKE MILK SAFER TO DRINK. INVENT A PROCESS THAT WILL DO SOMETHING USEFUL AND NAME IT AFTER YOURSELF.

NAME OF PROCESS: _____ IZATION

WHAT IT DOES: _____

_____

326.

THE CHEMICAL FORMULA FOR WATER IS H_2O. EACH MOLECULE OF WATER IS MADE UP OF TWO HYDROGEN (H) ATOMS AND ONE OXYGEN (O) ATOM. ADD FACES, ARMS, AND LEGS TO THIS OXYGEN ATOM AND ITS TWO HYDROGEN FRIENDS!

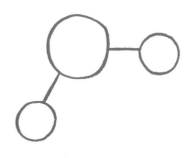

327.

HAVE YOU EVER WONDERED WHY IT DOESN'T HURT TO CUT YOUR HAIR? IT'S BECAUSE THE HAIR IS ALREADY "DEAD" WHEN IT EMERGES FROM THE FOLLICLES (LITTLE PITS) ON YOUR HEAD. GIVE THESE HEADS SOME FUN HAIRSTYLES.

328.

WHY ARE LAB COATS WHITE? THE WHITE MAKES IT EASIER TO SPOT ANY CHEMICAL OR LIQUID STAINS. GIVE THIS LAB COAT SOME COLORFUL STAINS.

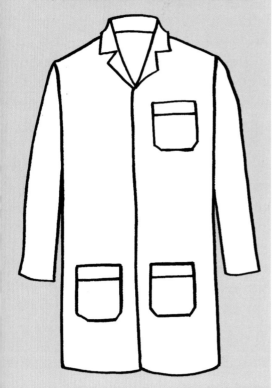

329.

DID YOU KNOW THAT EATING TOO MANY CARROTS (ABOUT 10 PER DAY FOR A FEW WEEKS) CAN GIVE YOUR SKIN AN ORANGE TONE? WHAT COLOR WOULD YOU GET FROM EATING YOUR FAVORITE FOOD?

FAVORITE FOOD: _____

_____

_____

COLOR: _____

_____

_____

330.

MEXICAN FARMER DIONISIO PULIDO WAS SURPRISED TO FIND A MOUND GROWING IN HIS FIELDS IN 1943. IT TURNED OUT TO BE A VOLCANO! IMAGINE YOU DISCOVER SOMETHING EXTRAORDINARY GROWING IN YOUR BACKYARD. WHAT IS IT?

331.

WHEN PHOTOGRAPHY WAS INVENTED, THE FIRST PHOTOGRAPHS COULD ONLY BE PRINTED IN BLACK-AND-WHITE. THINK OF A PHOTO YOU MIGHT TAKE—PERHAPS OF YOUR PET OR A FAVORITE TOY. DRAW IT IN BLACK-AND-WHITE IN THE FIRST FRAME AND IN COLOR IN THE SECOND FRAME.

332.

A KNOT IN A PLANK OF WOOD SHOWS WHERE A BRANCH ONCE GREW WHEN IT WAS A TREE. DRAW WHAT THIS WOODEN STOOL MIGHT LOOK LIKE IF ALL OF ITS KNOTS WERE STILL BRANCHES!

333.

YOUR BODY'S ORGANS EACH HAVE A SPECIAL JOB. FOR EXAMPLE, YOUR HEART PUMPS BLOOD AROUND YOUR BODY, AND YOUR LUNGS LET YOU BREATHE. MAKE UP A NEW ORGAN AND DESCRIBE WHAT IT DOES. BE AS SILLY AS YOU LIKE!

NAME OF ORGAN: _____

_____

WHAT IT DOES: _____

_____

_____

_____

334.

HUMANS ARE OMNIVORES—WE CAN EAT BOTH PLANTS AND MEAT. IF YOU COULD ONLY EAT PLANTS OR MEAT, WHICH WOULD YOU RATHER?

335.

A NONAGON IS A SHAPE MADE OF NINE SIDES. DRAW A NONAGON HERE.

336.

FOOD COLORINGS ARE DYES
THAT CAN BE USED TO
CHANGE THE COLOR OF FOOD—
LIKE MAKING ORANGE JUICE
GREEN! DRAW YOUR FAVORITE
FOOD OR DRINK, THEN COLOR
IT AN UNEXPECTED COLOR.

337.

PLACE YOUR HAND ON THE PAGE WITH YOUR FINGERS SPREAD OUT,
THEN CLOSE YOUR EYES AND DRAW AROUND IT, TRYING NOT TO
TOUCH IT. YOU SHOULD BE ABLE TO SENSE WHERE YOUR HAND IS,
EVEN THOUGH YOU CAN'T SEE IT! THIS IS CALLED PROPRIOCEPTION.

338.

TORNADOS ARE STRONG, WHIRLING WINDS THAT TRAVEL AT HIGH SPEED. THEY CAN UPROOT TREES, AND LIFT THINGS OFF THE GROUND. DRAW SOME THINGS THAT HAVE BEEN PICKED UP BY THIS TORNADO.

339.

IMAGINE YOU GROW UP TO BE A SCIENTIST AND WRITE A BOOK ABOUT YOUR WORK. FILL IN THIS COVER WITH YOUR NAME AND THE BOOK'S TITLE.

340.

MOST PEOPLE ARE RIGHT-HANDED. SOME PEOPLE ARE LEFT-HANDED. A FEW ARE AMBIDEXTROUS—THEY CAN USE EITHER HAND EQUALLY WELL. TRY WRITING YOUR NAME WITH EACH HAND. WHICH IS EASIEST?

341.

A PIE CHART IS A CIRCLE SPLIT INTO SEGMENTS TO SHOW HOW A SET OF INFORMATION IS DIVIDED. THIS PIE CHART SHOWS HOW THE HOURS OF THE DAY ARE DIVIDED UP INTO DIFFERENT ACTIVITIES. MAKE A NEW PIE CHART, SHOWING HOW YOU'D DIVIDE UP THE HOURS IN YOUR PERFECT DAY!

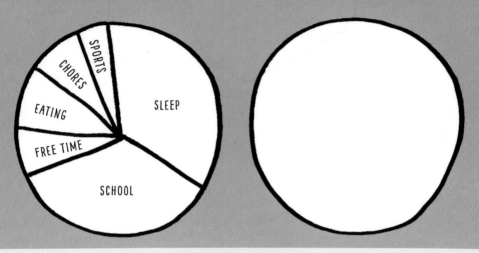

342.

IN AN ACROSTIC POEM, THE FIRST LETTER OF EACH LINE SPELLS A WORD. WRITE AN ACROSTIC POEM USING THE WORD "SCIENCE."

S

C

I

E

N

C

E

343.

SOME PEOPLE THINK THAT EATING CHEESE GIVES YOU BAD DREAMS, BUT SCIENTISTS HAVEN'T FOUND ANY PROOF OF THIS. DRAW WHAT THIS MOUSE IS DREAMING ABOUT AFTER EATING A CHEESE DINNER.

344.

SUBMARINES CAN DIVE THOUSANDS OF FEET BELOW THE SURFACE OF THE OCEAN. THEY HAVE BEEN USED TO INVESTIGATE THE SEABED AND OBSERVE SEA CREATURES. IMAGINE YOU'RE ON A SUBMARINE TRIP. WHAT DO YOU SEE?

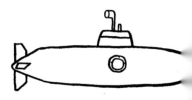

345.

IN THE PAST, PEOPLE USED POCKET WATCHES TO TELL THE TIME. THESE HAVE BEEN REPLACED BY WRISTWATCHES AND, MORE RECENTLY, BY CELL PHONES. HOW DO YOU THINK PEOPLE WILL TELL THE TIME IN THE FUTURE? WRITE OR DRAW YOUR IDEAS.

346.

THE HUMAN TONGUE CAN DETECT FIVE BASIC TASTES: SWEET, SALTY, SOUR (LIKE LEMON), BITTER (LIKE COFFEE), AND UMAMI (SAVORY AND MEATY). INVENT A NEW TASTE!

347.

NAILS ARE USEFUL TOOLS, USED TO SECURE THINGS TOGETHER. ANCIENT EGYPTIANS USED NAILS THOUSANDS OF YEARS AGO, AND IT'S POSSIBLE THEY WERE USED EVEN BEFORE THEN. DRAW A NAIL FOR THIS HAMMER TO HIT!

348.

A TSUNAMI IS A LARGE WAVE THAT FLOODS THE LAND. THEY ARE NORMALLY CAUSED BY UNDERSEA EARTHQUAKES. JUST BEFORE A TSUNAMI STRIKES, THE SEA DRAWS BACK, LEAVING SEAWEED AND EVEN FISH STRANDED ON THE BEACH. WHAT HAS BEEN LEFT BEHIND ON THIS BEACH? DRAW WHAT YOU MIGHT SEE.

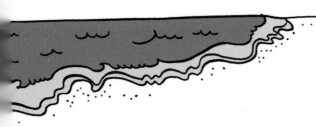

349.

THE PERIODIC TABLE SHOWS ALL OF THE 118 KNOWN CHEMICAL ELEMENTS, SUCH AS OXYGEN, IRON, AND CARBON. THERE ARE NO ELEMENTS THAT BEGIN WITH THE LETTERS J, Q, OR W. MAKE SOME UP!

J _ _ _ _ _ _ _ _ _ _ _ _ _ _ _

Q _ _ _ _ _ _ _ _ _ _ _ _ _ _ _

W _ _ _ _ _ _ _ _ _ _ _ _ _ _ _

350.

SNAILS NEED TO KEEP THEIR SKIN MOIST—THAT'S WHY THEY STAY HIDDEN WHEN IT'S DRY AND COME OUT AFTER RAINFALL. DRAW SOME TEENY SNAILS HERE.

351.

SLEEPWALKING, ALSO CALLED SOMNAMBULISM, IS WHEN SOMEONE GETS UP WHILE THEY ARE ASLEEP AND WALKS AROUND OR DOES OTHER ACTIVITIES. IT HAPPENS IN A PARTICULAR STAGE OF SLEEP. IMAGINE YOU ARE SLEEPWALKING—WRITE ALL THE THINGS YOU MIGHT GET UP TO!

352.

IF SOMETHING IS TRANSPARENT, IT MEANS YOU CAN SEE THROUGH IT. GLASS, PLASTIC, AND WATER CAN ALL BE TRANSPARENT. WHAT WOULD YOU DO IF YOU COULD BE TRANSPARENT FOR ONE HOUR?

_____

_____

_____

_____

_____

_____

_____

_____

353.

BRIGHT SUNLIGHT CAN DAMAGE OUR EYES. DESIGN SOME WACKY, DARK SUNGLASSES TO KEEP YOUR EYES SAFE IN SUMMER.

354.

THE SCOTTISH INVENTOR JOHN LOGIE BAIRD INVENTED THE TELEVISION IN 1926. THE FIRST MOVING IMAGE SHOWN WAS A RECORDING OF HIS BUSINESS PARTNER. WHAT WOULD YOU HAVE SHOWN IF YOU'D INVENTED THE TELEVISION?

355.

EYEBROWS STOP RAIN AND SWEAT FROM RUNNING INTO OUR EYES. WE ALSO USE THEM TO SHOW HOW WE FEEL. DRAW EYEBROWS ON THESE FACES TO SHOW THREE DIFFERENT EXPRESSIONS: ANGRY, SURPRISED, AND PUZZLED.

356.

IN THE FUTURE, IT MAY BE POSSIBLE TO VISIT PLACES IN SPACE AS A TOURIST. DESIGN A TICKET FOR A TRIP TO THE MOON.

357.

A PLACEBO IS A "PRETEND" MEDICAL TREATMENT—FOR EXAMPLE, A PILL MADE OF SUGAR. THE WEIRD THING ABOUT PLACEBOS IS THAT SOMETIMES THEY ACTUALLY WORK, AND THE PERSON TAKING IT FEELS BETTER! INVENT A PLACEBO PILL TO CURE ANYTHING YOU LIKE, SUCH AS A BAD MOOD.

NAME OF PILL: _

_ _

WHAT IT CURES: _ _ _ _ _ _ _ _ _ _ _ _ _ _ _ _ _

_ _ _ _ _ _ _ _ _ _ _ _ _ _ _ _ _

_ _ _ _ _ _ _ _ _ _ _ _ _ _ _ _ _

358.

VETERINARY SCIENCE DEALS WITH TREATING AND PREVENTING ANIMAL DISEASES. SOME VETS WORK WITH PETS, OTHERS WITH FARM ANIMALS, ZOO ANIMALS, OR IN THE WILD. IF YOU WERE A VET, WHERE WOULD YOU MOST LIKE TO WORK? WHY?

PET VET PRACTICE   FARM   ZOO   IN THE WILD

(CIRCLE YOUR ANSWER)

REASON WHY: _____

_____

_____

_____

359.

AN EARTHQUAKE IS A VIOLENT SHAKING OF EARTH'S SURFACE. MOST EARTHQUAKES ARE SO SMALL YOU CAN'T EVEN FEEL THEM. FINISH THIS STORY ABOUT AN EARTHQUAKE.

I WOKE UP SUDDENLY. MY BED WAS SHAKING! _____

_____

_____

_____

_____

_____

_____

360.

A MNEMONIC IS A TOOL THAT HELPS YOU REMEMBER A SEQUENCE OF WORDS. FOR EXAMPLE, "NEVER EAT SOGGY WAFFLES" HELPS YOU REMEMBER THE ORDER OF THE COMPASS POINTS: NORTH, EAST, SOUTH, WEST. MAKE UP A MNEMONIC TO REMEMBER THE ORDER OF THE PLANETS: MERCURY, VENUS, EARTH, MARS, JUPITER, SATURN, URANUS, NEPTUNE.

M _ _ _ _ _ _ _ _

V _ _ _ _ _ _ _ _

E _ _ _ _ _ _ _ _

M _ _ _ _ _ _ _ _

J _ _ _ _ _ _ _ _

S _ _ _ _ _ _ _ _

U _ _ _ _ _ _ _ _

N _ _ _ _ _ _ _ _

361.

WHEN SOMETHING FLOATS, IT IS DESCRIBED AS "BUOYANT." DRAW SOMETHING FLOATING ON THE WATER.

362.

THE FIRST EMOJI WAS INVENTED IN JAPAN. THESE LITTLE PICTURE SYMBOLS ARE USED TO COMMUNICATE EMOTION. DESIGN A NEW EMOJI.

363.

THE TRACKS ON TIRES AND THE PATTERNS UNDERNEATH YOUR SNEAKERS ARE DESIGNED TO GRIP. A SMOOTH TIRE OR SHOE WOULD SLIP ON A SMOOTH SURFACE. DESIGN A PATTERN FOR THE SOLE OF THIS SNEAKER.

364.

WHEN YOU SPEND A LONG TIME IN WATER, YOUR FINGERS WRINKLE BECAUSE THE BLOOD VESSELS IN THEM SHRINK. DRAW AROUND ONE OF YOUR FINGERS AND ADD LOTS OF WRINKLES!

365.

ALCHEMISTS WERE EARLY CHEMISTS. MANY OF THEM HOPED TO FIND A WAY TO TURN OTHER METALS INTO GOLD, BUT THEY NEVER SUCCEEDED. IMAGINE YOU SOLVED THE MYSTERY! HOW DID YOU DO IT?

First American Edition 2022
Kane Miller, A Division of EDC Publishing

Copyright © 2022 Quarto Publishing plc

Published by arrangement with Ivy Kids Co-editions, an imprint
of The Quarto Group. All rights reserved. No part
of this book may be reproduced, transmitted, or stored
in an information retrieval system in any form or by
any means, graphic, electronic, or mechanical,
including photocopying, taping, and recording,
without prior written permission from the publisher.

For information contact:
Kane Miller, A Division of EDC Publishing
5402 S 122nd E Avenue, Tulsa, OK 74146
www.kanemiller.com

Library of Congress Control Number: 2021949987

ISBN: 978-1-68464-452-0

Manufactured in Huizhou City, Guangdong, China. TT072022

1 2 3 4 5 6 7 8 9 10